⟞ The Sawdust Trail ⟝

T0108894

The Sawdust

A Hot Shot.

Yours Truly
W. A. Sunday

A Bur Oak Book

Trail

Billy Sunday in
His Own Words

By William A. "Billy" Sunday

Foreword by Robert F. Martin | University of Iowa Press, Iowa City

University of Iowa Press, Iowa City 52242
http://www.uiowa.edu/uiowapress
Copyright © 2005 by the University of Iowa Press
All rights reserved
Printed in the United States of America

The Sawdust Trail was originally published serially in the
Ladies' Home Journal in September, October, November,
and December 1932 and February and April 1933.
Reprinted courtesy of the Meredith Corporation.

Design by April Leidig-Higgins

Photos of Billy Sunday provided courtesy of Joseph M. Sanford

No part of this book may be reproduced or used in any form or by any
means without permission in writing from the publisher. All reasonable
steps have been taken to contact copyright holders of material used in
this book. The publisher would be pleased to make suitable arrange-
ments with any whom it has not been possible to reach.

The University of Iowa Press is a member of Green Press Initiative
and is committed to preserving natural resources.

Printed on acid-free paper

Library of Congress Cataloging-in-Publication Data
Sunday, Billy, 1862–1935.
The sawdust trail: Billy Sunday in his own words / by William A.
"Billy" Sunday; foreword by Robert F. Martin.
p.   cm. — (A Bur Oak book)
Book was originally published serially in Ladies' home journal,
Sept.–Dec., 1932 and Feb. & Apr. 1933.
ISBN 0-87745-949-5 (pbk.)
1. Sunday, Billy, 1862–1935.   2. Evangelists—United
States—Biography.   I. Title.   II. Series.
BV3785.S8A3 2005
269'.2'092—dc22
[B]   2005041751

05 06 07 08 09 P 5 4 3 2 1

Billy Sunday

Many years ago, when we had a meeting in Bellingham, Washington, we were invited to go to see some of the dense, virgin timber forest of that region, and, oh my! how dense they were. . . . There were men whose job it was to go into this dense forest and scale the timber . . . and when they finished their work they were to come out and report. . . . They carry great big, long sacks of sawdust with ropes around them. . . . As they pass from one spot to another, they reach in these sacks of sawdust and take a big handful and swish it along ahead of them where they're going, and they keep doing that every little while, making a sawdust trail from where they enter into the forest to where they stop at night, finish with their work, and are ready to go back home. So one of the men, through with his work, will say, "Well, I'm ready to go home. I'll be all right if I can just hit that sawdust trail." . . .

Well, Billy had been preaching for seven or eight nights in Bellingham without giving an invitation, and finally he decided that it was time to give one. And, as people started to go forward and take Billy's hand to accept the Lord Jesus Christ as their Savior, some man spoke up aloud in the meeting and said, "Oh, they're hitting the sawdust trail." . . . And the newspaper the next morning had a headline saying that a certain number of people hit the sawdust trail in the Billy Sunday Tabernacle the night before. That was the first time we had ever heard it used in connection with people accepting the Lord Jesus as their Savior. But we weren't surprised to hear them using it when we went to Everett, the next town where we held meetings in Washington, thirty or forty miles south of Bellingham, because that was in the lumber district, too. But we were surprised when it came back east with us, and it even got as far as New York City, and all the other big cities that we went to . . . every place we went it was called "hitting the sawdust trail," and we never got away from it.

—Helen "Nell" Sunday, *Ma Sunday Still Speaks*, pp. 25–27

~ Foreword ~

ROBERT F. MARTIN

William Ashley "Billy" Sunday was the best-known evangelist in America during the first half of the twentieth century. From 1896 to 1935, the controversial preacher toured first the Midwest, then the nation, preaching to between eighty and one hundred million people a version of the gospel that some found appealing and others appalling. Secular critics scorned or ridiculed the methods and message of the flamboyant revivalist, while those of a liberal, religious bent criticized what they regarded as the exclusivity, obsolescence, and provincialism of Sunday's ministry. Even some conservative evangelicals had misgivings about his unorthodox methods, but millions of his contemporaries regarded him as God's unconventional messenger to a sinful world.

Sunday's unconventionality was a matter of style and not substance. The intricacies of theology actually mattered little to him, but such doctrine as he espoused conformed largely to a few basic tenets of fundamentalist dogma. He took for granted the mainstream social and economic orthodoxy of his native region, and he equated the evangelical moral code of rural and small town mid and late nineteenth-century Iowa with Christian conduct.

Where Sunday deviated from the accepted norms of the day was in his manner of delivering the gospel. He was a gifted showman at a time when options for entertainment were far more limited than those of today, and there is no doubt that his showmanship was an integral part of his appeal. As thousands of enthralled worshipers watched, the former professional baseball player acted out the stories of the Bible, adopted a pugilistic stance as he challenged the Devil and his minions to battle, and mimicked the drama of the diamond by running, jumping, hurling unseen baseballs, and sliding for home plate. Yet, Sunday's success rested on more than his theatricality or even the conservative theology and conventional social norms that underlay his message. While both style and socioreligious doctrines were crucial to his success, another important reason that the revivalist was able to reach millions of his contemporaries was the perceived congruence between his life and work and the hopes and fears of people struggling to cope with the myriad of uncertainties inherent in their nation's rapid transition from a rural, agricultural society to an urban, industrial one. The revivalist's message spoke to their desire for continuity, while his life and ministry represented both a link with tradition and the possibilities inherent in change.

Billy Sunday was born in Story County, Iowa, near the present city of Ames, on November 19, 1862. He was the youngest of three sons born to William Sunday and Mary Jane (Jennie) Cory. Married in 1856, the couple struggled in vain throughout the late 1850s and early 1860s to achieve a measure of financial security. The realization that the military wage of thirteen dollars a month would help to keep the wolf from his family's door may well have contributed to William's decision to enlist in the Union Army in the late summer of 1862. He left for the war in September, before Billy's birth. In late December, William died of disease at a camp in Missouri, never having seen his new son.

The death of her husband left Jennie Sunday in desperate financial straits. Opportunities for widows to make a decent living on the Iowa frontier in the 1860s were limited. Consequently, it is not surprising that in 1864 she married James M. Heizer, a man almost twenty years her senior. Whether this was merely a marriage of convenience, or one of love as well, is not clear. What is certain, however, is that it was a mistake. Heizer was a poor provider, never bonded with his stepsons, suffered from alcoholism and, in 1871, finally abandoned his family, leaving Jennie, who now had four children, virtually impoverished. Following Heizer's departure, the three Sunday brothers continued to live with their mother, but for reasons that are not entirely clear, a guardian was soon appointed for them. In the fall of 1874, either their mother or their guardian placed the two younger Sundays, Howard Edward (Ed) and William (Billy), in the state orphanage at Glenwood, one of three homes established by Iowa for the orphaned children of Civil War soldiers. The following year, when the Glenwood orphanage closed, its residents, including the Sunday brothers, moved to a more commodious facility at Davenport. The orphanage experience was bittersweet for Billy. He disliked the separation from family and friends around Ames, but he also learned the discipline and some of the skills that would serve him well in his later years. Shortly after Ed and Billy went to Glenwood, their disabled older brother, Albert, became a resident of the Story County poor farm, where he lived for the next ten years.

In September 1875, Jennie married George Stowell, an itinerant laborer from Boone, Iowa. This union may have been emotionally gratifying, but it provided neither financial stability nor an opportunity for the reunification of Jennie's scattered family. In 1876, Ed and Billy returned to Ames and stayed for a short time on the farm of their grandfather, Martin Cory. It is not clear whether Jennie Stowell was living in the area at the time of her sons' return, but it is certain that, regardless of her whereabouts, her boys found themselves in difficult circumstances. Sixteen-year-old Ed soon got a job on a neighbor's farm and, later in the year, following a dispute with Cory, fourteen-year-old Billy moved to the town of Nevada, the county seat of Story County, where he worked first as a general factotum in a local hotel and then got a job doing household chores and caring for livestock for Colonel John Scott, former lieutenant governor of Iowa and prosperous Nevada resident. The Scotts were good to Billy and, while living in their home, he received a solid high school education, although he fell a few credits short of graduating. He also became acquainted with a comfortable and respectable side of middle-class midwestern town life, with which he had only limited prior experience.

During his senior year of high school, Sunday left Nevada for Marshall-town in nearby Marshall County. Several Marshalltown residents had heard of Billy's prowess as a runner and sought his services in their fire department, not because of his potential skills as a fireman but because they believed he would enhance the town's competitiveness in fire company competitions, a popular expression of the rivalry common among small midwestern communities in the latter nineteenth century. Sunday also played on Marshalltown's local baseball team, eventually coming to the attention of Adrian ("Cap") Anson, a Marshalltown native and professional baseball player who managed A. G. Spalding's Chicago White Stockings, the premier team of the fledgling National League. In the spring of 1883, Anson invited Sunday to come to Chicago to try out with the White Stockings. While the young Iowan was at best a mediocre batter, he was a respectable fielder and an extraordinary base runner. Anson was sufficiently impressed to invite him to join the club and, over the next five years, Billy became a popular and valued second stringer with professional baseball's most prestigious team.

In addition to his success as a professional athlete, Sunday's years in Chicago were marked by two other important developments in his life — a profound religious experience and his marriage. The place and time of Billy's born-again experience have been the subject of debate among

Sunday scholars, but Billy himself claimed that it began on a summer afternoon in 1886, when he and fellow ballplayers sat on a street corner in Chicago and heard the music of a roving band of gospel musicians and the preaching of a street evangelist named Harry Monroe. Monroe invited his audience to attend services at Pacific Garden Mission, a former beer garden transformed into one of the Midwest's earliest urban rescue missions. Sunday accepted the invitation and, after several visits, had a religious experience that eventually transformed his life, first from baseball player to YMCA worker, then to professional evangelist.

Following his conversion, Sunday began attending services at Jefferson Park Presbyterian Church, where he met Helen "Nell" Amelia Thompson, an attractive eighteen-year-old who was active in the youth work of the church. Nell was the daughter of William Thompson, owner of one of Chicago's pioneer dairy products businesses. Thompson objected to his daughter's association with a professional baseball player, since many had unsavory reputations. Despite her father's misgivings, Nell continued to see Billy secretly. Finally, the couple overcame paternal objections and were married in September 1888.

The Thompsons provided Sunday with something of an entrée into the world of urban, middle-class America. They were, by comparison with Billy, educated and refined, possessing the middle-class respectability to which he aspired. He also found in Nell and her family a psychological anchor that gave him the sense of emotional security he had lacked throughout much of his life. Furthermore, the Thompsons' involvement in the activities of the Jefferson Park Presbyterian Church undoubtedly strengthened Sunday's new and fragile commitment to Christianity.

Nell Thompson had an enormous impact on Billy and was instrumental in his later success. She was intelligent, strong-willed, practical, and stable, her personality complementing perfectly his rather insecure and

mercurial disposition. Throughout the forty-seven years of their marriage, "Ma," as Billy called his wife, would play the role of a surrogate
mother as much as that of lover and companion. She coached her husband
in the manners of the middle class, managed his business affairs, shielded
him from many of the stresses of everyday life, and brought order, security, and a measure of tranquility to his world.

In 1888, Billy joined the Pittsburgh Alleghenies, where he enjoyed
modest success as a first-string player. During his years at Pittsburgh,
he became increasingly active as a speaker and volunteer worker for the
YMCA and began thinking more and more about the possibility of full-
time Christian work. In late 1890, he was traded to the Philadelphia baseball club and completed the season there. Over the winter, he asked for
his release from Philadelphia to begin working for the YMCA in Chicago.
After initially rejecting Sunday's request, Philadelphia's management
released him from his contract in March 1891. For the next two years,
Sunday worked as an assistant secretary of the Chicago YMCA. In 1893,
he became an advance man with Presbyterian evangelist J. Wilbur Chapman, from whom he learned much about the fundamentals of revivalism.
When, in late 1895, Chapman retired temporarily from evangelism to
become pastor of Bethany Presbyterian Church in Philadelphia, Sunday
faced an uncertain future. He considered a return to baseball but abandoned the idea when he received an invitation, arranged by Chapman,
to conduct a revival in Garner, Iowa, in early 1896. His first evangelistic
endeavor was a success, and he quickly began receiving calls to preach
in other small towns in Iowa and Nebraska. Thus began one of the most
remarkable evangelistic careers in American religious history.

Throughout the first decade of his ministry, Sunday traveled what
he dubbed the "kerosene circuit," preaching largely in the small communities of the Midwest. After 1907, he began conducting revivals in

larger towns and cities, not only in the heartland but in other parts of the nation as well. During the 1910s, he preached to millions in most of the nation's largest urban centers, reaching the zenith of his career with a ten-week crusade in New York City in the spring of 1917. After World War I, changing social conditions, coupled with Sunday's deteriorating health and the debilitating emotional impact of the sexual entanglements and financial problems that plagued his sons, took their toll on the evangelist's ministry. Throughout the 1920s and 1930s, revivals became shorter, press coverage less extensive, and crowds smaller to the point that the large wooden tabernacles characteristic of his earlier ministry virtually disappeared. He remained popular in the towns and smaller cities of the South and Midwest, but his appeal in the cosmopolitan centers of the nation waned.

Sunday attributed his success not only to the will of God but also in part to his use of what he believed to be the most up-to-date business methods in his ministry. He developed an appealing product in the form of dramatic sermons encompassed by carefully selected music, skillfully used the press to advertise his work, and created a sophisticated organization to manage his revivals.

Just as good business practices generated expanding markets and handsome profits in the world of commerce and manufacturing, so too they appeared to contribute to a growing national demand for Sunday's services as an evangelist. With success came a commensurate rate increase in Billy's income. At the zenith of his popularity in the late 1910s, his urban campaigns generated enormous sums by the standards of that day. He donated a part of this substantial revenue to public causes, but a considerable portion of the "love offering" collected at the end of each revival went into his personal bank account. Sunday biographer Lyle Dorsett has estimated that between 1908 and 1920, when the average worker's wages totaled approximately $14,000, the evangelist earned more than one million dollars. Homer Rodeheaver, Sunday's popular, longtime chorister, claimed that by 1920 Dun and Bradstreet had estimated his boss's net worth at around $1.5 million.

Many observers found Sunday's materialism shameful, his flamboyance unappealing, and his message both antiquated and detrimental to constructive economic and social change. Millions of others, however, admired the way in which his sophisticated organization, skillful use of the press, businesslike methods, and unabashed affluence resonated with the business ethos of the day. Whether scorned or respected, Billy Sunday was one of the best-known men in America from the 1910s to the 1930s.

As his ministry expanded out of the towns of the Midwest into urban America, Sunday became the object of a great deal of popular curiosity. After 1907, he was the subject of numerous articles in secular as well as religious periodicals. Newspapers, especially those in areas where he was preaching or about to preach, gave the man and his ministry extensive coverage. During the 1910s, several authorized and unauthorized biographies appeared capitalizing on Billy's popularity. Sunday himself conveyed bits and pieces of his life story in interviews, sermons, and published writings, such as his 1915 volume *Burning Truths from Billy's Bat*. It was not until very late in his career, however, that Sunday agreed to write a firsthand account of his life and ministry. The fruits of his labor appeared as a serialized autobiography in the *Ladies' Home Journal* in late 1932 and early 1933. The autobiography is hardly a classic, as memoirs go, but it is pure Billy Sunday. The evangelist was first and foremost a preacher and, in some respects, wrote the way he preached. His sermons were never tightly organized expositions targeting the intellect. Rather, they were casual, anecdotal, melodramatic performances crafted to hold the attention of audiences and to appeal to the common sense of the average American. Billy's account of his life and work, like his sermons, is loosely organized, selective, episodic, and didactic, but it is also interesting and illuminating. It must, however, be read with a critical eye. Like Benjamin Franklin's more famous personal narrative, Billy's autobiography sometimes shows us what he wishes to have been, rather than what actually was. Fallible memory can plausibly account for some of the exaggerations, inaccuracies, and omissions in his portrayal of his life; however, he clearly chose to emphasize some facets of his story and to exclude certain significant episodes and individuals, as he created for himself a usable past consistent with the image of the hardworking, righteous, patriotic, successful, muscular Christian he wished to convey.

Sunday's account of his childhood in Story County is illustrative of his selective memory. He begins his narrative with the forlorn observation, "I never saw my father." These words are revealing. The absence of William Sunday, or of a viable surrogate, did much to shape Billy's personality and perspective on the world. No one ever adequately filled the void in his life left by William's death. His treatment of his stepfathers in the autobiography makes this quite clear. He dismisses James Heizer with only the brief observation that his mother married a man whom he disliked and that, consequently, he spent much of his childhood with his grandparents. He tells us nothing of the alcoholism, abandonment, or divorce that led to the fragmentation of the family. As for his mother's third marriage, to George Stowell, he neither acknowledges the union nor mentions Stowell. How these marriages may have complicated Sunday's relationship with his mother can be only a matter of conjecture. Neither the autobiography nor any other extant evidence provide many clues. In later years, Sunday tended to idealize the relationship, but it is difficult to escape the suspicion that as a child he felt some measure of rejection because Jennie, for whatever reason, made choices that did little, if anything, to create a stable family life for her sons.

Similar omissions occurred in Sunday's recollections of his maternal grandfather, Martin Cory. He was the closest thing Billy had to a surrogate father. In the autobiography, he recalls fondly his youth on his grandparents' farm and extolled Cory's virtues as a hardy and skilled frontiersman who was generous, community spirited, and an able provider for his family. The only hint of difficulty between Cory and his grandson is the story of Billy's abrupt departure from the family farm following an incident in which an enraged Cory swore at Billy and his half brother for damaging a harness. There is no reason to doubt that Sunday genuinely admired and loved his grandfather, but circumstantial and fragmentary evidence from other sources suggests that here too the relationship was more complex and problematic than Sunday would have us believe. As Martin Cory aged, his financial resources dwindled, and the necessity of continuing to provide for two of his Sunday grandsons, especially after their return from the orphanage in 1876, may have been the source of some resentment. This may explain why both brothers found employment elsewhere within a few months of their return to Story County. Another probable source of strain was Cory's occasional bouts of drunkenness and physical abuse of family members. Billy did acknowledge that his grandfather sometimes drank too much, but in his public writings there is no hint of the episodes of drunken abuse and sober remorse that Billy disclosed in a letter to Nell Thompson during their courtship. Obviously, these relationships had been problematic and, because they were either painful or embarrassing memories, he chose to disclose as little information about them as possible. Such reticence about familial discord is understandable, but it leaves the reader of the autobiography with a skewed picture of Sunday's childhood and obscures some of the factors that shaped his psyche.

There is, however, much in the autobiography that is of value to anyone wishing to know not only more about this extraordinary individual but also about the times in which he lived. Sunday's narrative provides an interesting glimpse into rural and small-town life in the Midwest in the 1860s and 1870s. He sometimes romanticizes the world of his youth, but he also hints at the dissonance between the harmonious, egalitarian, democratic ideal and the reality of familial discord, class distinction, and even a bit of town prejudice toward the country folk. He describes the hardships and harshness of that life as well. The story of his parents' and grandparents' mixed success as they struggled to extract a living from the Iowa prairie in the mid nineteenth century was hardly unique to the Sundays and Corys. Neither was the fragility of life that Billy portrays almost incidentally. In the twenty-first century, we insulate ourselves from death as much as it is possible to do so, but Sunday makes clear that for nineteenth-century Americans it was an integral and intimate part of everyday life. We see a distraught child lying in the snow atop the grave of his beloved grandmother. We share the family's sense of dread as a whippoorwill, an omen of death, flies into the room of Billy's terminally ill Aunt Elizabeth. We see a child deeply grieved over the loss of pets that had afforded a measure of companionship and security in a world plagued by illness and death.

Sunday's narrative also reflects another characteristic of late nineteenth-century life, that of migration from the farm to the towns and cities of urbanizing, industrializing America. For Billy, as for millions of his contemporaries, it was an exciting transition full of possibilities for the future but one fraught with anxiety as well. In his case, it provided opportunities that would dramatically change his life. The base paths were Sunday's avenue out of the rural Midwest and into the teeming streets of urban America. It was his play on the diamonds of the fledgling National League that first made him a visible part of the American scene and, for some readers, his description of his career as a professional athlete may be the most appealing part of the narrative. Billy's recollections suggest the rather casual nature of professional baseball in the late nineteenth century. It was a game with little equipment, minimal coaching, and no organized farm system, but there are also hints that already the sport was becoming more and more professional. His story of the sale of the White Stockings star Mike "King" Kelly to Boston for ten thousand dollars or his account of White Stockings owner A. G. Spalding's hiring of a detective to keep an eye on his undisciplined team suggests a game in which players, who once enjoyed a status something like that of independent artisans, were becoming subordinate to a management class that exerted considerable control over contracts and the workplace.

It was not, however, the business of baseball but the game itself that captured Sunday's imagination. The autobiography makes it very clear how much he loved the game. Forty years after he stowed his uniform and spikes, he still vividly remembered the exciting games and spectacular plays in which he had been involved. To be sure, he sometimes exaggerated his prowess as a hitter. He was in truth a mediocre batter, with a career average of .256, but he played the outfield with abandon and was a daring and phenomenally fast base runner. His skill, enthusiasm, and clean-cut image made him a popular figure with the fans of the teams on which he played. Nothing, not even his fame and success as a preacher, ever wholly eclipsed those years in which he heard the approbation of the crowds as he sprinted after line drives, raced around the base paths, or made spectacular catches.

Although Sunday retired from active play in his late twenties, his years in baseball remained an integral part of his public image and enhanced his appeal, first as a YMCA worker and then as a professional evangelist. The game provided him with a wealth of metaphors and anecdotes with which to enliven his sermons and a means by which he could more easily reach the hearts and minds of audiences. His accounts of asking divine assistance, as he strove to make the difficult play, conveyed his faith that God was an ever-present help in time of trouble. His stories of some of his former teammates cast them in the roles of principals in a kind of morality play, in which their wasted lives served to suggest the consequences of sin, and his own success gave testimony to the rewards of salvation and the consecrated life.

Billy's career in baseball facilitated his evangelistic success in at least one other way. It lent an aura of manliness to his ministry. At the end of the nineteenth and dawn of the twentieth century, many Americans worried about the loss of the manly virtues among the nation's youth. Some Christians were especially concerned about what they feared was the feminization of American Protestantism. No one could doubt, however, that Billy Sunday, the former baseball player, was a man's man. His athleticism in the pulpit, as he mimicked play on the diamond, astonished and amused audiences. The fact that he had been an athlete lent an aura of authenticity to his stories of risking personal harm to confront unworthy husbands or of chasing an assailant who attacked him during one of his earlier revivals. Even in the autobiography, the first installment of which was published when he was seventy, we still sense Sunday's desire to portray himself as a healthy, happy, muscular Christian, willing to take on the Devil and his minions at every opportunity. He had conveyed this image throughout his career and, in doing so, he affirmed for millions of American males that Christian manliness was the most noble expression of masculinity.

Sunday's decision to leave professional baseball ultimately brought him fame and fortune far in excess of anything he had known on the diamonds of the National League, but his extraordinary success also made him susceptible to a great deal of criticism. Much of it he brought upon himself because of his penchant for stylish cars, expensive clothes, the company of the rich and powerful, and his generally affluent lifestyle as he became a nationally known figure. Billy considered material success a sign of God's favor, and criticism irritated him. It is not surprising, therefore, that he often emphasized the early sacrifices he made for the sake of his faith. He reminds us that he gave up a guaranteed annual salary in excess of $2,000 with the Philadelphia ball club for a precarious one of $1,000 with the financially strapped Chicago YMCA. He recounts the hardships of his early days as a solitary revivalist, enduring meager accommodations, the discomforts of train travel, the challenges of tent revivalism, and the occasional ingratitude of local parishioners such as those in one small town who gave Billy only $33.00 for a two-week campaign. Fortunately for the modern reader, his efforts to parry those who criticized his wealth and success provide an illuminating glimpse into the life of the urban YMCA worker and the small-town midwestern evangelist around the turn of the twentieth century.

Yet, Sunday was more than God's messenger to the nation's heartland. He was ultimately a national figure who, though controversial, had broad appeal for millions of his contemporaries. Billy attributed much of his success as an athlete and evangelist to the blessing of God, a contention that eludes the conventional tools of historical analysis, but his autobiography suggests several more mundane and tangible reasons for the revivalist's remarkable accomplishments. Much of Billy's appeal lay in the way his life and work resonated with a number of important themes in American life. We encounter in these pages a man who triumphed over youthful adversity and adolescent hardship to become a player in the nation's favorite sport and then to emerge as the leading preacher of his era. His life and work were, therefore, consistent with and validated the American myth of success. We meet a tough, courageous fighter for righteousness, who took on crime, vice, immorality, and demon rum in a combative spirit, reminiscent of the stereotypical image of generations of two-fisted frontier preachers.

At the same time his life was firmly rooted in national myths and traditions, Sunday's ministry responded to important changes occurring in industrializing, modernizing America. In a nation that increasingly craved entertainment, Billy was a gifted showman. He instinctively knew how to use music, humor, melodramatic stories, extraordinary athleticism, and the plain speech of the common people to manipulate audiences to achieve desired ends. In an age in which the rhetoric of democracy was pervasive, he tried to portray himself as just "plain" Billy Sunday. In his account of his ordination examination, for instance, there is a touch of both self-effacing humor and anti-intellectualism, as he tells readers that when asked about one of the giants in the history of the church, he responded that if Augustine did not play in the National League, he knew nothing about him. Sunday had no qualms about reducing his methods and message to the lowest common denominator to reach the masses. As he tells us, "I put the cookies and jam on the lower shelf so an audience don't have brain fag when they sit and listen to me."[1]

Sunday's unabashed patriotism, sometimes little short of chauvinism, was another feature that played well to audiences proud of their nation's growing power and prestige in the early years of the twentieth century. His sorrow over, but pride in, the sacrifice his father had made for the sake of the Union tugged at the heartstrings of a nation that romanticized the Civil War and venerated those who fought in it. Likewise, congregations thrilled to his rabid attacks on Germany during the "Great War" and responded generously to his appeals on behalf of the government's Liberty and Victory Bond campaigns. Billy was, for them, a true-blue American who scorned cowardice, ridiculed radicalism, and extolled the virtues of the American way of life.

One feature of American life which permeated his ministry was the business mystique of the early twentieth century. Indeed, he believed that the church's failure to apply the methods of the contemporary business

~ The Sawdust Trail ~

I never saw my father. He walked from Ames, Iowa, to Des Moines, thirty miles, to enlist in the Civil War, and was assigned to Company E, Twenty-third Iowa Infantry, in August, 1862. I was born on my grandfather's farm one mile south of Ames, Story County, Iowa, the nineteenth of the following November.

My father was born near Chambersburg, Pennsylvania, and was of Pennsylvania Dutch parentage. He was a contractor and brick mason by trade, and built one of the first brick buildings ever erected in Cedar Rapids, Iowa.

He sleeps in an unknown grave beneath the eternal flowers and the perpetual sunshine of the Southland, waiting for the trumpet of Gabriel to sound the reveille on the Resurrection morning. Then, for the first time, I shall look into the face of him whose name I bear, and whose blood courses through my veins.

> No more the bugle calls the weary one;
> Rest, noble spirit, in your grave unknown.
> I shall see him and know him among the brave and true
> When a robe of white is given for his faded coat of blue.

His regiment forded a river which was partly frozen. He and scores of other soldiers caught severe colds that caused complications from which he and many others died. They were buried at Camp Patterson, Missouri, but all trace of the graves has been blotted out.

I have had the War Department and private investigators at various times try to locate father's grave, but all efforts have failed. Thousands of soldiers' bodies were removed by the Government and reinterred in the Government cemetery at Jefferson Barracks, near St. Louis.

— The Old Log Cabin —

While conducting a campaign in that city a few years ago, I visited Jefferson Barracks. I stood with uncovered head amid the thousands of graves of known and unknown Union soldiers, and prayed for the living relatives of the heroes, thinking that perhaps dad sleeps there under the protecting folds of Old Glory.

When I started out to preach I was, and still am, the uncompromising foe of the forces that crush human hearts, blight lives, feed the flames of lust and passion, brutalize their minds with opiates, sell their souls for rum and cause them to sow the seeds that produce the harvest of misery for themselves and tears of sorrow for their loved ones. I show that, though sowing wild oats may have a kick in it, it is the harvest that brings a curse to the sowers and tears of sorrow to father and mother.

Because I do this, the forces of corruption and evil that feed and fatten and gormandize on human weakness saw that my buckshot style of preaching tore off the mask and revealed the hideous face of the devil and the fruits of sin, causing hundreds and thousands to forsake their evil ways, and flee to God for forgiveness and salvation.

All sorts of willful and malicious lies were started and circulated against me, some even going so far as to say that my father was not a soldier, and that I trumped up the story to appeal to the sympathy of the people. I sent to Des Moines to Adjutant General Guy E. Logan and had him send me the official record of dad's enlistment and death, to shut the mouths of the blatant liars.

Father wrote to mother from the front lines and said, "When the baby is born, if it is a boy, name him William Ashley." So my name is William Ashley Sunday. I was born in a log cabin and lived there for years until my grandfather built a sawmill, run by water power, cut lumber from black-walnut logs, and built a frame house which stands today on the old farm near Ames.

The city of Ames and the county of Story were named after the families of Ames and Story, who lived in Boston and were among the capitalists who helped build the Chicago & Northwestern Railway, whose main line from Chicago to Omaha runs through Ames.

My grandfather was one of the men who helped locate the Iowa Agricultural College at Ames, now named Iowa State College. He had no money to give with which to start the college, and so he gave part of his land as his donation. He and two other men, pioneers of Story County, Dan McCarthy and L. Q. Hoggett, aided in staking out the ground and locating the first building of what has become one of the greatest schools of its class in the United States.

He and General Grant were second cousins. Both were born in Ohio. After General Grant became President he wrote a letter inviting grand-dad to visit him in Washington, but it was a long, tiresome journey in those days, and expensive, too, and money was as scarce as mosquitoes in January.

Granddad wore a coonskin cap, rawhide boots, blue jeans, and said "done hit" instead of "did it," "come" instead of "came," and "seen" instead of "saw." He drank coffee out of his saucer and ate peas with his knife. He had no "soup-and-fish" suit to wear, so he did not go.

During the first three years of my life I was sickly and could scarcely walk. Mother used to carry me on a pillow which she made for that purpose. There were no resident physicians in those pioneer days, and itinerant doctors would drive up to our cabin and ask, "Anybody sick here?"

One day Doctor Avery, a Frenchman, called at our cabin and mother told him, "I have a little boy three years old who has been sick ever since he was born."

The old doctor said, "Let me see him." He gave me the once-over, while I yelled and screamed like a Comanche Indian. Then he said to mother, "I can cure that boy."

She asked him how much he would charge, and he replied, "Oh, if you will feed me and my old mare, that will pay the bill."

Mother said, "All right; but you will have to sleep up in the garret. We have no stairs and you'll have to climb the ladder."

— The Country Doctor —

He replied, "That suits me." He then went into the woods and picked leaves from various shrubs, including mulberry leaves and elderberries, dug up roots and from them made a sirup and gave it to me. In a short time I was going like the wind and have been hitting on all eight ever since. From that day to this, elderberries and mulberries have been my favorite wild fruit, and I like sassafras tea.

I do not believe there is a disease to which human flesh is heir but that somewhere there is growing a weed or an herb or plant that will cure it. Somewhere there is a remedy for the dread plagues of the human race, consumption and cancer. God has made the cure and is waiting for man to discover it.

The greatest doctor this world ever knew is an old Christian mother, and my mother was the greatest of all. I regret that she did not write down the names of all the herbs and roots she knew, and the diseases they would cure. When she put on her "specs" to look at the sore and spread salve on it, that made it almost well.

You may name this suggestive therapeutics or the power of mind over matter. All these designations are as useless as the name of the horse that Paul Revere rode. The fact remains.

My mother was born in Syracuse, Kosciusko County, Indiana. Her maiden name was Mary Jane Cory. She was the oldest of a family of eight children and she outlived them all. Her parents moved to Story County, Iowa, in 1848. They were three months making the journey. There were no bridges and they would often camp for a week waiting for the water in the rivers and creeks to fall so they could ford the stream. They lived on deer, wild turkey, ducks, geese, bear and fish. Their home was the covered wagon, their cookstove the campfire. Today a fast airplane could make the trip in two hours.

Grandfather was the second man to take up Government land in Story County. Mother helped clear the land, grub stumps, crop corn, plant potatoes, milk the cows, yoke the oxen, harness horses, plow the fields, chop wood, hive the bees, cook. I say, I believe she could beat the world making biscuits, buckwheat cakes, flour gravy, and cooking raw-fried potatoes.

As civilization developed, the churches and schools came. Mother's two younger sisters were well educated and taught school. The education which is rewarded by diplomas and scholarship was not mother's, although in native shrewdness, born of contact with Nature, she was miles ahead of her sisters.

⎯ My Grandfather ⎯

Mother married again some years after my father died. I didn't like the man whom she married and I went to live with my grandparents. We all lived on the same farm. Then my stepfather died, and mother came to live with grandfather.

These are days of specialists in all professions. In the legal profession one is a corporation lawyer, one a patent lawyer, one a criminal lawyer. The human anatomy is divided into sections. The day of the old practitioner is passé, like the old family album, the oxcart, candles, and hoop skirts.

But my grandfather was the most versatile man I have ever known. There was seemingly nothing that he could not make. He made wagons, the wheels and all parts of them. He could build houses and lay stone walls. He made a turning lathe and made bedposts, spindles for banisters, made bureaus, water wheels and many other things.

He had a blacksmith shop and made horseshoes and wedges with which to split wood. He could dress a millstone on which to grind corn and wheat. Before he built the mill for sawing lumber and grinding grain, he and the neighbors had to drive to Burlington, two hundred miles away, to mill. He made all the ax handles sold by the hardware stores in Ames.

He made a loom upon which grandmother spun yarn and made cloth, from which she made dresses and cloth for suits. My clothes were made from homespun until I was sent to the Orphans' home. While the clothes were ill-fitting affairs, they were warm. You couldn't tell from looking at my pants whether I was going or coming.

In those days, when people were sick, they used to bleed them by lancing a vein in the left arm because it was near the heart and would bleed more profusely. Grandfather had a spring lance and had nerves of steel and he was always sent for to perform the operation.

He gave a plot of ground, beautifully located on the bank of the river, and covered with oak and elm trees, for a cemetery. Hundreds are buried there, but the graves are grown over with trees and they could not be located by any research. The old family burying ground is there, and ten of the family sleep beneath the trees. I have cared for the graves for more than thirty years.

I remember one night a fellow named Sam Brandon, who lived in Ames, came bursting into our home, knocking the latch off the door as he came. He was pale and trembling, and screamed, "There's a ghost down at the graveyard. I saw it trying to jump out of a grave."

Grandpa got a lantern and we all went down there. We kids went with fear and trembling and clung close to grandpa. We found a grave that had been dug for a funeral the next day, and one of our sheep had fallen in the grave and was trying to jump out. He would get far enough above the top so you could see his head and shoulders, and then he would fall back in. The supposed ghost proved to be a sheep, which we rescued.

When we were fighting for the Eighteenth Amendment, some scoundrels went to the farm, which was then owned by Captain Greeley, of Ames, and asked if my relatives were buried there. They were informed that they were.

Those black-hearted degenerates, so vile that the devil would duck up an alley to avoid meeting them, went to the graves, tore down the fence I had built, tipped over the gravestones, threw brush on the graves, and took photographs and had them published in whisky-sympathizing papers. Under the photograph was the caption, "This is the way Billy Sunday takes care of the graves of his relatives." I wish I had been there! Some of them would have gone away in the Red Cross wagon.

Grandfather made all the coffins after he built the sawmill. They were all made of black walnut, which grew in abundance in the forest.

He was a great provider. The cellar was always filled with apples, potatoes, barrels of sauerkraut, salt pork, corned beef, and molasses made from sugar cane. The cabbage and parsnips and turnips we buried out-of-doors and dug them up as needed. The garret was filled with rings of dried pumpkin, dried apples — peeled and quartered and strung on a string, dried sage, peppermint, catnip, red peppers, dried beef, and a supply of candles, for we used candles until kerosene lamps came into use.

Our house was the stopping place for visiting strangers. Everybody was welcome.

Newspapers were scarce, although the country editor, with his Washington hand press and grip filled with type, was only a step behind the pioneer. The newspaper was our bible.

The press is the mold in which public opinion is cast. It is the scepter that directs the course of public thought. There was a time when the platform and the pulpit were masters of men, but today there has arisen a power mightier than an army of orators, a power that has overshadowed their genius and dwarfed their influence. When the press arose, the orator diminished.

No man is more indebted and more grateful than I to the newspapers for their aid in helping me to spread the gospel to millions who have never seen my face. No one can see more quickly through a fraud, or rise more quickly to genuine sincerity, than newspaper men and women. I have never had one double-cross me. My prayer for forty years has been, "God bless the newspaper editors and reporters, typesetters, and the office devil, and the newsies who sell on the streets."

I used to help milk ten cows night and morning. We had one old cow, a Hereford, that could open the gate with her head, and when we tied the gate with a rope she would untie the knot with her horns and lead the whole herd into the cornfield. I can hear the call to round up the night raiders, "Oh, boys, get up! The cows are in the corn." My, how I did hate that white-faced cow, and how happy I was when the butchers got her.

I kept up my station in the harvest field with men when only eleven years old. That was before the days of the McCormick self-binder, when the grain was cut with a foot-dropping reaper; and we bound a bundle with a band we made from the grain. I can make that band today as quick as you can bat your eye.

I know all about the dark and seamy side of life. If you knew the hardships and struggles and mountains of difficulties I have climbed, and the distance I have come, you would be surprised that I do as well as I do. A great deal of our criticism of others is cruel and unjust, because it does not take into account the distance they have journeyed and the obstacles surmounted in order that they may be where they are. As my friend, the late Elbert Hubbard, said, "If you wish to avoid criticism, be nothing, do nothing, say nothing."

Most every farmer planted a patch of sugar cane from which to make sorghum molasses. Grandpa made a cane mill. He cut down sycamore trees from which he made the rollers. There were three rollers. The master roller was twice as long as the others and had a long, curved sweep to which we hitched a horse that went round and round to grind the cane we fed into the mill. We were the only ones that had a cane mill, so all the farmers would bring their cane to us.

We had to keep the juice from each farmer's cane separate, and boil it separate until it became molasses. We would do the work gallon for gallon, giving them one and keeping one. Or, if they wanted to pay for it, we charged twenty-five cents per gallon. Often we would have to work until midnight, for we could not leave the sap once we put it into the vat to boil. We had to skim off certain residue that the boiling would bring to the surface.

— Tricks —

One night, after grandfather had drawn the vat of molasses off the fire and was waiting for it to cool to barrel it, he sat leaning against a tree, dozing. He was awakened by a noise of something falling. He opened his eyes, sat up, and there was a big black bear licking molasses from the iron kettle which he had upset. Grandfather had left his rifle leaning against a tree fifty feet away, so he grabbed a stick from the fire and hit the bear.

The bear grunted "Woof, woof" and started to run. Grandfather hurled the stick and it struck the bear and the live coals fell off in the long hair of the bear. He rushed for his rifle and fired at the sparks for a target, but the bear escaped.

We would get hungry and make a raid on the hen roosts for a fat chicken. We would draw the chicken, then cover it, feathers and all, with wet clay, then bake it in the hot coals and ashes. Nothing is more delicious than fowl and potatoes cooked this way. "Them days is gone forever," but their memory lingers still.

I was the favorite grandchild with both my grandparents, perhaps because I was the last grandchild. Grandfather taught me many gymnastic tricks. I could ride a horse bareback standing up. He and I would ride the horse to town, I standing on grandpa's shoulders, and we would parade down Main Street, while everybody looked with open-eyed wonder at the free performance.

One time when Adam Forepaugh's circus came to town, I was one of a hundred boys who were there to watch them put up the big top and carry water for the camels and elephants, and I showed my bag of tricks. Forepaugh wanted me to go with him. He said he would make a great performer out of me.

Colonel John Scott, the lieutenant-governor of Iowa, with whom I lived, dealt in Shetland ponies. He bought them by the carload. I used to break them, and would pick out some special ones I liked and train them to perform. I built a springboard and practiced until I became so proficient that I could turn a somersault over an old cow and three ponies lined up. I always stood the old cow next to the springboard.

One day an itinerant photographer came to our house and everybody said, "Oh, let's have Willie's picture taken." They placed me in a high-chair, and when the photographer set up his camera and drew that black cloth over his head to get the focus, and pointed the lens at me, I became frantic. I screamed in fright and jumped out of the chair. They placed me back in the high-chair, but I fought and screamed like a wildcat. They begged and scolded, coaxed and promised me candy. No use; I fought on. Finally the photographer said, "I can't stay here all day—hold him in the chair and let him yell." They did. Mother stooped behind me and held me while the fellow "turned on the juice," and when the picture was developed you could see mother's hands holding me, but no other part of her body could be seen.

One sight of that picture and the recollection of how they had put it over on me made me mad and I wanted to destroy it, for my face was a composite of that of Lon Chaney, Ben Turpin, Jackie Coogan and Charlie Chaplin. They kept that tintype hidden, because I had threatened to burn it. One day I found it and sneaked out and buried it in the snow; and when the spring sun melted the snow they found the picture. Then they had the goods on me. "Be sure your sin will find you out" is one of my favorite texts for a sermon.

The weather had faded the likeness so that it was almost blotted out, but time has not erased the incident from my memory, and I would give one hundred dollars if I had that old picture now.

~ Billy Pig ~

We had a pet otter named Jeannette. She was trained to catch fish and would bring them up on the bank of the river and lay them down. She would come to the house wet, from fishing, and climb on the bed and drag herself across the bed to dry. One day, trying to get a piece of meat

after the funeral my mother missed me. They called and searched everywhere; finally my dog picked up the scent and they followed my tracks through the snow to the graveyard, and there they found me lying across her grave, weeping and chilled through with the cold November winds. For weeks they feared that I would not live, but God spared my life and has led me where I am today.

The battle grew hard. The wolf of poverty howled and scratched at the cabin door. Mother decided to send Ed and myself to the Soldiers' Orphans' Home at Glenwood, Iowa. There were three such homes located in the state — Glenwood, Cedar Falls and Davenport. One of the saddest memories of my life is the recollection of the grief I felt when leaving the old farm to go to Ames to take the train for the trip to Glenwood. I had never been farther away from home than Nevada, the county seat, eight miles east.

When we climbed into the wagon to go to town I called out, "Good-by trees, good-by spring." I put my arms around my dog named Watch and kissed him. The train left about one o'clock in the morning. We went to the little hotel near the depot to wait. That hotel was left standing for forty years.

The proprietor awakened us about twelve-thirty, saying, "The train is coming." I looked into mother's face. Her eyes were red and her cheeks wet from weeping, her hair disheveled. While Ed and I slept she had prayed and wept. We went to the depot, and as the train pulled in she drew us to her heart, sobbing as if her heart would break.

The conductor called "All aboard!" and the train pulled out. We raised the window. With my arms outstretched toward mother I cried, "I don't want to go to the Orphans' Home. Take me back to the farm with you." And today something tugs at my heartstrings, saying:

I want to go back to the orchard,
    The orchard that used to be mine;
Where the apples are redd'ning
    And filling the air with their wine.

I want to wake up in the morning
    To the chirp of the birds in the eaves;
I want the west wind through the cornfields
    To rustle the leaves.

I want to run on through the pasture,
    And let down the dusty old bars;
I want to find you there still waiting,
    Your eyes blazing like the twin stars.

Oh, nights! you are weary and dreary;
    And days! there's something you lack.
To the old farm in the valley —
    I want to go back.

Shall I ever forget the home of my childhood? Yes: when the flowers forget the sun that kissed and warmed them. Yes: when the mountain peaks are incinerated into ashes. Yes: when love dies out in the human heart. Yes: when the desert sands grow cold.

— A Mother's Love —

The last sound I heard that memorable night was mother's voice crying "Good-by, boys," on the midnight air.

A mother's love is unselfish, and it has no limits this side of heaven. A mother's arms and a mother's heart are a safe anchorage for any boy. I do not believe there are devils enough to pull a boy or a girl out of the arms of a Christian mother.

It was my pleasure and privilege to provide a home for my mother during the last thirty years of her life. She died at our home at Winona Lake, Indiana, on Mrs. Sunday's birthday, June 25, 1918. I went to call her for breakfast that beautiful Sabbath morning and found that she had slipped away to heaven without bidding us good-by.

Some of us can remember our old-fashioned mothers. We see their forms and faces through memory's glasses, clad in homespun dresses, preparing the meals for those whom they loved. We hear them singing the old-fashioned songs as they tucked us in the old-fashioned trundle bed and we cuddled down to sleep under the protecting blankets; and we see them as they sat by the fireplace, as the sparks danced in poetic disorder up the chimney, and by the dim light of the tallow candle darned our socks, patched our pants, until midnight sent them off to bed.

We buried mother in the family lot on the old farm, by the side of her father and mother.

⁓ The Sunlit Hills ⁓

One of the brightest pictures that hang on memory's wall is the recollection of the days I spent when a boy on the farm. I went back years ago for a visit. I shut my eyes and visions of the past opened before me. I listened for the sound of voices forever still, and longed for the touch of hands turned to dust.

The man became a child again. The long, weary years of struggle and heartache became as though they had never been. Once more, with my gun on my shoulder and my dog at my heels, I roamed the woods, walked down the old familiar paths, sat on the old familiar stumps and logs. The squirrel barked defiantly from the limb of an oak tree.

I threw myself into an interrogation point, and when the gun cracked the squirrel fell at my feet. I grabbed him by the tail and dashed home and threw him at mother's feet and received compliments for my skill as a marksman. Once more I listened to the "tinkling bells that lulled the distant fold."

I saw the cows wind slowly o'er the lea, I saw the crows winging their weary flight to the darkening woods. I heard the whippoorwill sing his lonesome song way over in Sleepy Hollow.

I saw the shades of night creep on. I heard mother call, "Oh, boys, come in to supper." Once more I ate my frugal meal of mush and milk. Once more I knelt and lisped the prayer millions have prayed:

> Now I lay me down to sleep —
> I pray Thee, Lord, my soul to keep;
> If I should die before I wake,
> I pray Thee, Lord, my soul to take —
> And this I ask for Jesus' sake. Amen.

God likes to see a man leave the misty, fog-covered valleys and climb the sunlit hills. More people fail from lack of purpose than from lack of talent. Half the ills that curse the world come from eagerness to achieve success in realms you cannot reach. If fate clips your wings and casts you on the humbler plains of life, be a hero there. There is plenty of room for heroism in the common walks of life. Don't stand gazing at men while they fly their kites into the crags and peaks of financial speculation and worldly glory, and allow some fellow to pick your pockets of manhood and honesty and make you a liability instead of an asset to your family and your country.

The world is full of unsuccessful men letting empty buckets down into empty wells and drawing up nothing but hot air. You will get out of life just what you look for. The vulture sees the carrion, no matter how high he soars. The bee looks for flowers everywhere he goes; he gets the honey where the spider gets his poison.

Any fool can form a bad habit, but it takes a real man to break one. Every man has been knocked down once or twice, but it is the getting up that counts. Nobody will fall down twice on the same banana skin unless he is a fool. Character can no more be hid than you can hide fire in powder. Counterfeit character is more common than counterfeit money.

We reached Council Bluffs the next morning, tired, sleepy, cold, hungry and homesick. We wandered down the streets and saw a sign, "Hotel." We went to the back door and asked for something to eat. The lady asked, "What are your names and where are you from? Where are you going? Did you run away from the home?" She surely put us on the grill.

We replied, "Our names are Ed and Willie Sunday, and we're from Ames, and are going to the Soldiers' Orphans' Home at Glenwood. We didn't run away either. Here is our letter to the superintendent, Mr. Stephens."

She put her arms around us and said: "My husband was a soldier. He never came back. I never turned anyone away hungry, and I wouldn't turn you orphan boys away. Come in, Eddie and Willie."

We ate our breakfast. She did not put just so much on our plates, but put us about six inches from the table and let us eat until we touched. Oh, those buckwheat cakes and sausage, with sage ground in them! I can taste 'em now! We sat in front of the fireplace and soon fell asleep. About noon she awakened us and asked: "Boys, do you want some dinner?"

We replied, "Uh, huh."

After dinner we strolled over to the Burlington Railroad yards and saw a freight train being made up. We climbed into the caboose. When the train pulled out, the conductor came in and said: "Tickets!"

We said, "We ain't got no tickets."

He asked, "Where is your money?"

We replied, "We ain't got no money, Mr. Conductor."

He said, "I will have to put you off down at Pacific Junction."

— Kindness for the Friendless —

We began to cry. "Where are you boys going?" he asked. We said, "To the Soldiers' Orphans' Home at Glenwood. Our pa is dead." Then we handed him our letter of introduction from our guardian, Hon. Joe Fitzpatrick, state senator, of Nevada, Iowa.

He read it, and I saw the tears in his eyes as he handed back the letter, saying, "Sit still, boys; it won't cost you a cent to ride in my train."

That conductor used to visit the home to see his "boys," as he called us, and always had candy and nickels in his pockets for us. The Burlington Railroad had covered bridges in those days. There was such a bridge just east of Glenwood. One dark, stormy night, he was out on top of the cars, helping set the brakes — that was before they had Westinghouse air-brakes. He forgot to stoop to clear the bridge and his head struck the top crossbeam which crushed his skull. I wish I could remember his name so that I could visit his grave and place a wreath of flowers there.

I wonder how many realize what a kind act such as this means in the life of a poor, friendless boy, facing a cold, cheerless world that seems to care no more about him than a dead cat on the highway.

We remained at the home until the legislature of Iowa discontinued that home and the one at Cedar Falls, and combined all three in one big institution at Davenport. Mr. S. W. Pierce, superintendent of the home at Davenport, came to escort all the children whose parents wanted them transferred.

Those who wished them to return home were given that privilege.

Most of them went to Davenport. None of the children ever liked the new home so well as they did the old home at Glenwood. There we had the freedom of the fields and the woods that surrounded the home. The institution was ideal in its location. The land was of rolling hills and dales and dense forests of stately trees. Nuts of all kinds grew in abundance. Every Saturday we could go hunting squirrels and rabbits, play ball and run foot races. My granddad could outrun any young man in the county where he lived. I guess I inherited his speed, for I could do the same. I could outrun any boy in the Glenwood Home.

There were two boys older than I at Davenport, Frank Styles and Perry Howard, and it was nip and tuck between us three. Whoever got the start would win. That shows how closely we were matched for speed.

We had two dandy dogs that could tree squirrels and chase rabbits. They were pets with every child. When we left the home for Davenport we wanted to take the dogs with us, but the "powers that were" ruled against us and sentenced them to be shot. When we saw the man going into the woods with the dogs, we began to hurl our protest and plead for the dogs. When we heard the reports of the gun that told us our dogs were dead, we all cried. We hunted and found them and dug one grave and put the dogs to rest side by side, covered them with leaves and grass, and filled the grave. We never liked the man who shot them and would never speak to him unless occasion required us to do so.

To reach Davenport from Glenwood, you take the Burlington to Council Bluffs, then the Rock Island to Davenport. En route to Davenport you pass through Des Moines, the capital of the state of Iowa. It is only thirty miles distant from the old farm at Ames. My brother, Ed, and I had it all planned out. I was to jump off the train when it stopped. Ed was lame and could not run fast. I could run all day and never tire. I knew every curve in the road and figured I would be home by morning.

Ed confided to a chum and the "rat" squealed to Superintendent Pierce.

As the train neared Des Moines, he came and sat on the arm of the seat so that I couldn't make my get-away. I was heartsick and boiling mad at that kid, and the first chance I had I cleaned up on him.

— Punishment for Runaways —

If ever the state of Iowa had two public servants absolutely fitted for the responsible position of caring for its orphans, they were Mr. and Mrs. S. W. Pierce, superintendent and assistant superintendent of the Soldiers' Orphans' Home at Davenport, Iowa. They were as opposite in their temperaments and methods of dealing with the boys as winter is from summer. Mr. Pierce was stern and a stickler for rules and discipline. He used the rawhide on tough, unruly fellows.

Every spring, as sure as the grass turned green and the flowers bloomed and the birds returned, some of the boys would be seized with the wanderlust fever, and would set the stage for a get-away. Over the fence they would go like sheep, but he would follow them to the farthest confines of the state and bring them back. If a boy reached home he would bring him back, and if his folks wanted him home they would be required to place a formal request for his release according to the law.

He would bring the runaways back, and in front of the administration building was an oval park with a cinder driveway about an eighth of a mile around it. He would put the captured boys there and they would have to walk around and around that park for one week, starting every morning at eight o'clock, walk until noon, eat dinner, start at one, march until supper, and then come back for one hour after supper. Their feet would get so sore and their muscles so tired that they would almost fall over. No boy was allowed to speak to them until their term of "hitting the cinders" was finished.

Mrs. Pierce would talk to the boys, take them on her lap, and tell them how sad their mothers would be if they knew it. She would pray with them, and no one ever came from an interview with Mrs. Pierce dry-eyed. Any boy would rather have Mr. Pierce whip him than have Mrs. Pierce talk to him. Both are in heaven, but their memory blossoms sweet in the dust.

— Blacklisted at Meal Time —

At Glenwood, if you missed one meal without permission, you were compelled to miss the next meal as punishment. Believe me, the boys were usually there with the feed bag on.

The superintendent would tell the children what was going to be served — you as hungry as a wolf, and knowing you could only stand and watch the others. It was agonizing. He would read the names of those who were blacklisted for that meal, and they must stand during the meal.

Some kids would say, "Bill, do you want a drumstick?" Often they would pity you and take a long chance and sneak out a chicken leg; but if they were caught they had the same sentence passed on to them! That method of dealing with us had more effect than a wagonload of switches.

At both homes religion had an important place in our training. All our teachers and officers were Christians. I never knew a boy from either home to be an infidel or a criminal. Of those of whom I have kept track, some became lawyers, merchants, farmers, railroad men, educators. I was the only one who ever became a big-league baseball player.

We had prayers in each home once a day. On Sunday evenings, before we went to bed, each boy was required to recite a verse of Scripture. If he did not know a verse, he was given five demerit marks. Thirty demerit marks in a month would change your grade. You got three demerits if your face was not clean, three if you hair was not combed. Those who were detailed to make the beds received eight demerits if they failed to make them according to standard rules.

I was never in the bad grade, but I was often near the deadline. I had two strikes on me many times. As I look back, I wonder how I got by. I once got into a fight with the bully of a rival cottage, which would have put me "on the spot." But the gang stood by me, and we convinced the cottage manager that the other fellow started the scrap and I finished it, so I escaped.

There were five grades, 1, 2, 3, 4 and 5. Grades 1 and 2 were good. Grades 3, 4 and 5 were bad. Every boy and girl on entering the home was assigned to Grade 2, so it was up to you to advance or retrograde.

Those in grades 3, 4 and 5 were never allowed outside of the grounds. Those in good grades were allowed to go to Davenport on Saturdays and also to the city churches on Sundays.

All the merchants knew by our uniforms who we were, and they would give us apples, candy, pop corn and ice cream. That was an incentive to go straight. Only a certain number could go each week. Had the whole gang gone, we would have taken the merchants "to the cleaner's." We would line up in front of Superintendent Pierce and ask, "Can we go to town?"

"What grade are you in, boys?" he would ask. He always trusted us. I never knew a boy to lie about his grade. Then he would say, "Take off your hat," and if our hair was not combed, "Step out of the line," would be the command. That meant we "got the hook."

One more question, "Are your shoes shined? Turn and let me see the heels," and if they were not shined, you couldn't go. I never knew of a boy trained in that home that ever failed to shine the heels of his shoes.

We all dressed alike. Our winter suits were given us about October first. They were made of wool—a mixture of gray and brown, with four buttons straight down the front. The clothes for all the children were made by the older girls who were detailed to the sewing room. Our summer suits were made of denim, and the girls wore calico. On Sundays we all wore white collars with a little tie. Our shoes were square-toed, straight on both sides, so it made no difference which foot you put them on.

At Davenport they used the cottage system, with about twenty-five children in each cottage and a woman manager for each cottage. There were about thirty cottages. The superintendent and assistants and cottage managers and teachers, cooks and watchmen, in all made a faculty of 150 besides 600 or 700 children. The dining room was about half a mile from the cottages. The children marched in especially assigned divisions to their meals. No haphazard mob rush. There was a covered walk to protect us from the cold and storms.

Every Decoration Day all who were in good grades were taken for a ride on the Mississippi River, as guests of the Diamond Joe Steamboat Company, and then we were taken to the government island to decorate the graves of the Union and Confederate dead. This island was purchased by the Government and the arsenal established before the Civil War, when Jefferson Davis was Secretary of War. It is today Uncle Sam's greatest arsenal and military depot. Two hundred and fifty Confederate soldiers are buried there. They were sent there as prisoners of war, and the cold, damp air of the North mowed them down faster than Yankee bullets.

The Government cares for the graves, and of all the government cemeteries that I have seen, none surpasses the neatness and care bestowed upon the graves of the Confederate dead buried at Rock Island, Illinois. Carved over the massive stone entrance are the dying words of Stonewall Jackson: "Let us cross over the river and rest under the shade of the trees."

I have preached in every state in the South. I never heard anyone say harsh, vindictive words about General Grant. In a city in Georgia stands a hotel named Lee-Grant Hotel. I have never heard anyone in the North hurl epithets against Robert E. Lee. As the son of a Union soldier, I uncover my head to General Lee.

I was conducting a campaign in Columbia, South Carolina, and one day a committee of women representing the Daughters of the Confederacy, came to me and said: "Mr. Sunday, our fathers were all in the Confederate Army in the Civil War. Your father was a soldier in the Northern Army, and you never saw him; he died in the service. We have purchased a piece of ground in our cemetery and dedicated it to your father, and every Memorial Day we will put flowers there and keep the flag flying in honor of your father; and we will pass this pledge on to our children." Money cannot buy such friendship.

At the home we never went to the dining room for Sunday-evening supper. Attendants always brought our supper to our cottages. The supper for each child always consisted of a big piece of gingerbread, a piece of apple, peach, pumpkin or mince pie — in season — and an apple. The boys used to trade their pie or gingerbread or apple for some trinket, and some shrewd traders would have three or four pieces of pie or gingerbread coming to them each week. If the kid who owed him ate his portion without paying his debt, he would beat him up.

⸺ A Yarn Ball ⸺

I have known boys to have their Sunday-evening lunch traded for the month ahead. I would have been "sunk" many a time had it not been for my brother, Ed. He was detailed as assistant to the chef, and carried the keys to the pantry and would sneak me in and lock the door; and, oh, boy, I would make a hole in Uncle Sam's commissary department! In about fifteen minutes he would unlock the door and I'd beat it.

The age limit that boys could remain at the home was sixteen, girls eighteen. My brother had to leave because of that limit and I would not stay. We both left and went back to the only home we knew, grandfather's on the farm. Shortly after our return, Ed went to live with a neighbor who had no boys, a noble Christian man, named Cyrus Simmons. After staying there for years, he returned to the home as one of the carpenters and watchmen. He married one of the girls and they moved to North Dakota, where he entered land from the Government and worked for the Northern Pacific Railway Company.

Every child had some special work to do. I was assigned to the laundry. I became so expert that the lady manager had my length of time extended. We were detailed to one job for a short period, and then changed to another job. What I learned there opened the door in after years that has brought me where I am — I was taught to do my best. Do your best, that's all an angel can do. No one does his or her duty unless he does his best. More people fail from lack of purpose than from lack of opportunity. Their sparker and gas don't work together.

Little did I dream when I made me a yarn ball, and threw it in the air to see how far I could run and catch it, that I was training myself to become a member of the famous Chicago Cubs, and the Pittsburgh and Philadelphia baseball clubs of the National League.

One day on the farm, grandfather was in a hurry to go to town. We were helping him hitch up the horses. My half-brother, Roy, and I got hold of the neck yoke and were trying to pull it away from each other, and we pulled the rings out of the end. Grandfather was furious at our foolishness, as it delayed him. He swore at us and it cut me to the heart. I'm of a sensitive nature, and am still sensitive. I went to a neighbor's, Parley Sheldon, who for fifty years was a delegate to Democratic national conventions.

After we husked the corn on our grandfather's farm, my brother Ed and I used to husk corn for Parley Sheldon. We could husk and crib one hundred bushels a day. We received three cents a bushel — Ed took two dollars and I one dollar.

I borrowed a horse from Parley and rode to Nevada, the county seat, eight miles away to look for a job. I found a position working in a hotel. I swept out the office and on Saturdays mopped out the office and dining room, chopped the wood, milked two cows, cared for the stable and went to the trains. I was the "barker" for the "beanery." I would call out, "Welton House, fine eats, clean beds only two blocks away, and a dollar a day." I would carry the traveling men's grips to the hotel, and if they had sample trunks I would hitch up the team and drive to the depot and bring the trunks to the sample room. I used to sleep in the office behind the counter, and if anyone came in the night I would let them in and show them to their room. I was bellhop too.

The proprietor of this little hotel in Nevada had a trotting horse of which he was very proud. She was a beautiful animal, sorrel, with white face and four white feet, and her tail dragged on the ground. They used to take great pride in showing her off to visitors. I would put the halter on her and trot her down the road a hundred yards or so, putting one hand on her shoulder and taking hold of the halter with the other.

I became so proficient in speed for that distance that I could "run her off her feet" — that is, she would stop trotting and go into a run. That training gave me my speed and breath for one hundred yards. I could go that distance and never breathe. I was not what you call a long-distance runner, like Nurmi, the great Finn, although I could run three hundred yards in thirty-four seconds!

— Finding a Home —

I worked there several months and became homesick for the old farm and a sight of familiar scenes and faces. I was given permission to go home and stay one day. I stayed two days, and when I returned I was fired—given the gate.

The next day I learned that Col. John Scott, then lieutenant governor of Iowa, wanted a boy. I got my hair cut, shined my shoes as I had learned at the orphans' home, and went to see Colonel Scott. He was a dignified Scotchman. I told him who I was and that my father was a soldier, and I had been to the orphans' home. That got under his vest, and he said: "Well, Willie, you're a nice-appearing boy; but Sophy"—Mrs. Scott's given name was Sophia; he called her Sophy—"hires all the help, and you come back tomorrow and see her."

You bet I was back the next day—Johnnie on the spot. She asked me, "What can you do, Willie?"

I replied, "Anything, and if I don't know how, I can learn."

She smiled at that answer and asked, "Can you milk cows and chop wood?"

I replied, "Yes, ma'am, I can."

"Can you scrub the floor?"

"Yes, I can."

"I need a boy who can scrub floors and steps. It's so hard for me to get down on my knees." She was a fleshy woman. "Well, I'll try you out and see what kind of a job of scrubbing you can do."

I was foxy. I didn't tell her that was my long suit, for I had been taught that at the Soldiers' Orphans' Home, and had she asked me to pick out the job for a tryout, I would have chosen to "scrub the floor." There were fourteen steps leading into the cellar. She said, "I'll scrub the first step and show you how. You scrub the others, and then I'll decide." Little did she dream that I could scrub rings around her.

I was soon through with the steps and she was amazed that I did it so quickly. So she said, "Oh, you are like all boys, a lick and a promise. I'll wait until they dry." When she put her critical eye on them, she patted me on the shoulder and said, "You'll do. You are hired. Here is your room. Go get your clothes."

I said, "I got 'em all on." They became godfather and mother to me; they were educated and refined.

⎯ School Days ⎯

While I lived on the farm there moved into our neighborhood a man who came from New York State named Henry Christman. He bought land from my grandfather. He had come West for his health. He was highly educated — a college graduate of an entirely different type from the pioneers that surrounded him. It was not long before the school board recognized his superior learning and employed him as a teacher for our district country school. Boys and girls graduating from that school under his instruction were so far advanced that they could enter the junior class of the colleges.

So when Colonel and Mrs. Scott said to me, "We want you to attend school," I was all set and entered the Nevada High School. Speaking, geography, history and civil government were my long suits. "Horatius at the Bridge," "Curfew Shall Not Ring Tonight," "Spartacus to the Gladiators at Capua," "The Raven," "Rodger and I," and "The Arab's Farewell to His Steed" were among my favorites.

At the end of two years I applied to the school board for the position of janitor, and to my surprise and delight they gave me the job. I had to get up at two A.M. during the winter months and start the fire in the stoves. There were fourteen fires to build and keep going during the day. In addition, I had to study and keep my lessons up to standard. Many times I would fall asleep over my books. I had to sweep the building every day after school and dust every seat. I did all this and milked the cow and did the chores at Colonel Scott's home for my board.

There was one teacher that used to get on my nerves, and I presume I got on her nerves too. She would say, "Willie, if you don't dust these seats better than you are doing, I shall be compelled to report you to the school board."

I said to myself, "I'll fool you!" So I took a damp cloth and dusted everything neat and tidy, and when she came nosing for dust, she found none.

She said, "I'm proud of you. You are doing your work splendidly." She taught me to do a common thing in an uncommon way.

All some people care for is appearances. They are all front door — open the door and you are in the back yard. If all the tombstones told the truth, the devil would be wearing mourning.

Where gold has value, brass does its best to shine up and imitate it. Like an old lady who went into a jewelry store to purchase a piece of jewelry. She would lick every piece that was shown her, with her tongue. The jeweler remonstrated, "Madam, you can't tell gold that way."

She replied, "I know it; but I kin tell brass."

Sham battles don't kill. Sham character doesn't count. When you are doing the little things, you are qualifying to do the big things later on. The mockingbird will never learn to sing if he takes music lessons from a hoot owl. The spider is sure the bee is a fool. The hen thinks the duck has deformed feet. Ask a camel what the world is made of, and if he could talk he would say "Sand." Ask a whale, and he would say "Water." A sheep never finds out what frost is until he loses his wool. As the twig is bent the tree grows. The man does thus and so today because he did thus and so yesterday. It is because the young man goes in bad company that he dies an old man in the penitentiary.

Your success in life tomorrow will be determined by what you said "yes" or "no" to today.

I am asked about the young people in my youth as compared with today. I don't know that young people do things today they did not do when I was young. They have more ways of making fools of themselves.

There is no question that conditions have changed. I believe there are more slime pits and pitfalls and sidetracks to lure young people from the paths of righteousness than at any time since the Stars and Stripes have floated over our land.

No wonder we have a low standard of morals when men will write such sewage as appeared in a magazine recently. The author said that the physical familiarities which we call "petting" are normal and educational, and denied that "petting" was bad physically for young people.

What is there educational about being parked on an infrequented side-road with the lights out, a girl seated on your lap, your arms about her, and both filled with booze? You must be a moral idiot if you haven't brains enough to know that a "petting party" is a secondary sexual love feast, and that no normal boy or girl will escape; they will go to the limit.

— Yesterday and Today —

You can dot every hilltop in America with a red schoolhouse; you can erect a university in every teeming center of population, until ignorance will slink away like a wolf in a den; and yet America will sink into hell unless her purity of heart keeps pace with her brilliancy of intellect.

Then we have this companionate marriage bunk spread broadcast, which is further encouraging the young people to trample all moral standards in the mire. Companionate marriage is the marriage of the zoo and barnyard. All the monkeys, baboons and gorillas, hogs, cattle and cats live in companionate marriage, free to quit any time. If we have the sins of Babylon, we will have her judgments.

The strife of materialism has brought upon us the curse of present-day conditions. Modesty, loyalty and faith in God seem lost in the craving of the senses which appeal to the baser desires of men.

Girls permit liberties today which ten years ago would have been considered akin to immoral. Now they pass as clever. They are skating on thin ice, running on a flat tire.

There seems to be an increasing intimacy between the sexes. Each sex tries to blame the other; each is equally at fault.

By far too many girls are looking for easy spots; they are not willing to begin where their mother did—by the side of some good, honest poor boy.

If the girl who has lost her virtue is unfit to marry, the man who has lost his virtue is as unfit to marry as is the girl. To marry some is like a turtledove marrying a turkey buzzard.

Keep up the standards of your life.

Don't joke about religion.

Don't go to places of questionable amusements.

Don't allow men to use vulgar language in your presence.

Don't visit places about whose character you are not absolutely sure.

Don't marry to spite some other fellow.

A good woman is the best being this side of heaven; a bad woman is the worst being this side of hell.

Marriage may not always result in the happiness you had hoped for; maybe it's your fault; maybe it's her fault.

Love is something you cannot quarantine, vaccinate or reason with any more than you can reason with a bulldog with a bone.

In our garden on the farm we grew every vegetable that was native to that section, and we always had the seed planted early and were the first to have garden produce for sale. Granddad would give me half the proceeds of the sales. I would wash the vegetables at the spring and with a basket on each arm, filled with fresh vegetables, walk to Ames, one mile, and peddle them from door to door.

— The Town Nine —

I did this on Saturdays, as I went to school the rest of the week. Sometimes my share would amount to twenty-five or thirty cents, and I would spend it for lead pencils, candy or a rubber ball. Then on my way home, and when going for the cows, I would practice throwing the ball in the air great distances from me, then run and catch the ball. All through my career as a baseball player that was one of my assets. Because of my speed and ability to judge fly balls, I was the only country boy who played on the "town" nine. Whenever they had a game with some rival town nine, they always sent for me, and if I was working in the harvest field they would hire some man to take my place. Several professors from the college played on the town nine. Professor MacCumber played second base. Val Hoggett, now assistant editor of the *Denver Post*, played right field.

One day when I was peddling vegetables, I rapped on the kitchen door of a home in Ames and asked, "Do you want any vegetables? I pulled and washed them this morning; they are fresh."

The man of the house, after buying some, asked me, "Say, bub, do you know burdock when you see it?"

I replied, "Yes, sir; I know the name of everything that grows."

"Well," he said, "my wife is sick and the doctor told me to make her some tea out of burdock roots, and if you will bring me some I will give you a nickel."

"All right, sir," I answered. "I'll get them for you and bring them to you in a little while." And away I ran, for his purchase had emptied my basket of vegetables. I hurried home, one mile in the country. The river was out of its banks and the road in places was two feet under the water. I splashed through the flood waters, reached home, got a spade and dug up burdock roots enough to make three bundles, and back I hurried. I knocked on the same kitchen door. He came, and I said, "Here are your burdock roots."

He said, "Why, bub, I asked a boy after you had gone and he said he would bring me some, as there was a patch growing in their yard. He was here half an hour ago, and so I don't need yours."

I said, "You asked me first, and I've been away out to the farm for these roots."

He smiled factitiously and said, "The roots are on the stove cooking, so I can't use yours, little boy."

I boiled over and threw the roots at him and said, "Keep your old burdock. I won't sell you any more onions and radishes." And I never did. I never liked the man after that. He was a great church man, too, and after I became an evangelist, he used to drop into some of my meetings. He was a traveling man. He would give public testimony and say, "I knew Billy when he was a barefoot boy, and he used to sell vegetables to me that he raised on the farm and carried into town."

I used to say to myself, "Yes, you old skinflint, you owe me that nickel yet."

The Fourth of July was always ushered in with the booming of a cannon at the Iowa State College at sunrise, which was about 4:30 A.M. that season of the year. I was up at the first crack of the gun, did the milking and turned the cows out in the woods to pasture, grabbed a few mouthfuls of breakfast and beat it for town. I usually had twenty-five cents to spend, which I had saved from sale of vegetables. Soon the streets would be filled with people from the country who had come to celebrate the natal day of this, the greatest nation God's eye ever saw or His hand ever made.

Soon the refreshment stands would open for business and the barkers would begin announcing their wares to the crowd. One fellow with a voice like a megaphone would call out, "Right this way, la-dees and gen-tel-men, ice-cold lemonade, made in the shade, stirred with a spade — forty feet under the ground — only five cents — one-half of a dime."

I would blow myself to a glass, and it was real lemonade and a sure-enough glassful. Not these little dinky glassfuls that they sell today for fifteen cents or a quarter. I would buy a glass of lemonade, three cents' worth of sweet crackers, two cents' worth of bologna, a bunch of fire-crackers for ten cents, and a dish of ice cream for five cents, and then I would be broke.

One Fourth of July they had a free-for-all foot race, distance one hundred yards; prize, three dollars. Fourteen men entered. I was the only boy. I was keyed up for one hundred yards. Everybody was as excited over that as they are over football and world-series games. There was a professor from Iowa State College entered. He had on running shoes and a silk suit, rose-colored. Oh, boy, but he looked great to our calico-overall country eyes!

We lined up at the starting line. There was a log lying directly on the line. The distance was packed on both sides with spectators. I took my place on the outside with my right foot against the log as a booster. I took my shirt off, rolled up my overalls to just below my knees. I ran bare-footed.

The starter — a fellow with long whiskers — called out: "Get on your mark — get ready — go!"

Away we flew. At twenty-five yards half the bunch were "washed up." At fifty yards all were through except the college professor, a long-legged farmer boy named Bates and myself. At seventy-five yards Bates was all in, and the silk-decked professor and I were side by side. Oh, how my farmer boy friends did yell, "Go it, Bill, go it!"

My teeth were set as if I had the lockjaw. My fists were clenched. Above the shrieks and screams of the mob I heard my granddad, who was near the tape, say, "Go it, son, go it, son!" I shot ahead of the professor and beat him by five feet. The boys picked me up and carried me on their shoulders and yelled, "Bring on your college professors. We can beat the bunch."

— Volunteer Fireman —

I rushed up to town to the Fourth of July treasurer, a merchant named Soper. A gang of kids followed me. I burst into the store and said, "Mr. Soper, I want the three dollars for winning the foot race."

He said, "Oh, go on. That was a man's race. The boys' race will come later on."

I said, "Yes, but it was a free-for-all, and I beat the college professor."

Just then a member of the amusement committee came in and said, "Yes, this boy won the free-for-all. Give him the money." He gave me three silver dollars and I treated the gang to lemonade and ice cream. I was a millionaire for a few hours.

When the boys' race was called, I stayed out because a boy friend of mine could outrun all the others except me. He won the race and collected one dollar.

The next attraction was to catch and hold a greased pig. They shaved the hog — he weighed about one hundred and twenty-five pounds — and greased him with oil and melted lard. Then they turned him loose. I took after him with the others and away we went. Some would grab him by the legs and their hands would slip off and away would go the pig. I got close to the hog and threw my arms under his neck and hung on for dear life. I brought the pig to a standstill and was declared the winner. I got the dollar prize, so we country jakes, as the town boys called us, cleaned up on the prizes that famous Fourth.

There were no paid fire departments in Iowa those days. All were volunteer and composed of picked men, mostly young men. Each year there was held a state tournament. Some city would invite the fire departments and offer prizes for various contests, such as foot races, climbing a ladder and hose-company races. The rivalry between cities for the championship of the state was terrific.

The contesting cities would fine-tooth-comb the country for fast runners. They searched for them like the big leagues do for ball players today. They sent out scouts to look over the athletes at high schools and colleges. A scout came to Nevada and, after watching us play baseball and noting how fast I could run, came to me and asked if I would go to Marshalltown and join the Woodbury hose team. He offered to get me a job or pay my board if he failed in getting me a position. You were required to live in the city thirty days before you were eligible to run in the championship race. The state tournament was held the last of May, so I decided to go. I was in the senior class of the high school, but I left one month before the graduation exercises were held. Therefore I did not officially graduate from high school.

The principal event was the hose-cart race. The cart was a two-wheeled affair, with a drum on which to wind the hose. It had to weigh five hundred pounds. It had a tongue about six feet long with a crossbar at the end. Each company was allowed twelve men to pull the cart. We had to run three hundred yards from a standing start. At the end of the three-hundred-yard course a dummy hydrant had been erected. Each hose cart was required to carry one hundred feet of two-inch fire hose, coupled in fifty-foot lengths, that must be unreeled. We were required to couple one end to the hydrant and put the nozzle on the other end of the hose. The company that did all this in the quickest time won the championship.

An inch rope was fastened to the axle of the hose cart and ran through rings under the tongue, then long enough for ten men to be hitched to the rope. We had a crosspiece of hickory several feet long for a singletree. This was fastened to the inch rope. A man was snapped to each end of the singletree. We had a broad surcingle strap two inches wide back of our necks and under each arm and across our breasts for our harness.

The tournament that year was held in Muscatine. That city searched high and low for fast runners, and they had as members of their fire company M. K. Kettleman, Harry Bethune, both ten-second men, and Fred Stone, who years afterward became athletic director of the Illinois Athletic Club in Chicago. Those men were to the cinder path what Babe Ruth is to baseball and Earle Sande is on the back of a Derby horse. We drew "cuts" to see which team would lead, and we drew No. 1.

Everybody gasped when he saw our outfit go down the track and cover the three hundred yards in thirty-four seconds. The crack Muscatine team had never done better than thirty-six seconds in training. Our two men who were assigned to couple the nozzle on the hose at the end of the run became "shell-shocked" and instead of doing it in three seconds, their usual time, they took eight seconds, and we lost the championship by two seconds. We were all sick. The thought of losing that cup by two seconds kept constantly surging through our minds like a fire pressure.

I went back to Marshalltown and got a job working in a furniture store. I learned to finish furniture and to make mattresses. The firm had to deliver all the furniture sold, and I took care of the team and drove the delivery wagon when not working in the finishing room or making mattresses. There was an undertaking department connected with the store, and when anyone purchased a coffin they always sent the hearse to the funeral. I was always assigned to drive the horses. I didn't like that part of my job. I couldn't stand the grief and sorrow of the people mourning over their departed loved ones, and to this day I do not like to visit a cemetery or attend a funeral, and I never see a funeral procession that I do not remove my hat and offer a prayer that God will comfort those left behind.

— My First Telegram —

I played baseball on the local Marshalltown, Iowa, team. We cleaned up on all clubs against whom we played. Finally Des Moines challenged us for a game for five hundred dollars a side and all the gate money, to decide the championship of the state. Some Marshalltown men put up the five hundred dollars. Among them was Mr. McFarland, editor and publisher of the *Times-Republican*, who afterward became director of all the United States consuls in Europe.

We won the game 15 to 6. I played left field. Des Moines had some heavy right-handed sluggers, and our captain figured that I could get the fly balls. I had eight put-outs and made six of our fifteen runs.

Pop Anson, captain of the famous Chicago White Sox, of the National League, now the Cubs — years ago they changed the color of their stockings and Ban Johnson and Charles Comiskey organized the present American League and placed a rival club in Chicago, and Comiskey decked his team out with white stockings and named them the "White Sox," but the Cubs were the original White Sox — used to spend many of his winters in Marshalltown visiting his parents and relatives. His father, Henry Anson, gave an entire block in the heart of the city to the county commissioners upon which to build a courthouse, and a magnificent and stately court-house stands there today.

I believe Cap Anson was beyond doubt the best batter, take him year in and year out, that ever walked up to the plate. He used a heavy bat — the limit in both length and weight. He could hit 'em high or low, in or out. He was the hardest man for a pitcher to fool, as we say. He faced men who were the equal of any of the great pitchers today in speed, cunning and curves.

I remember one season when Cap struck out only four times.

Cap and Mike Kelly were always kidding each other, and when Cap went to the bat the last time in that particular season, Mike said: "Cap, I'll bet you fifty you strike out."

Cap would back his judgment on any proposition, and said, "You're on!" And I'll be horn-swoggled if he didn't strike out — making his fourth strike-out for the entire season.

When Cap came to Marshalltown one winter everybody was praising my ability as a ball player, how fast I could run, and because of my speed could catch fly balls that no one else would even attempt; but that seemed only an incident in his daily conversation.

Cap had an aunt. We called her Aunt Em. She always attended ball games and had gone to Des Moines with the hundreds who went along to root for us in that championship game, and she had watched that game and knew the part I had in helping to win the championship. She was enthusiastic and kept urging Cap to take me to Chicago for a trial.

He did not promise that he would, but after he had returned to Chicago in the spring, he telegraphed for me to come on for a tryout. That was the first telegram I had ever received and was it good news!

I gave up my job with the furniture company, finishing furniture, making mattresses and driving the hearse, and got ready for the trip. I bought a new six-dollar suit of sage-green color. I borrowed money for the trip. I had been drawing $3.50 a week from the furniture job and paying three dollars a week for my board, so you can easily figure out that I knew nothing about Bradstreet and R. G. Dun. I reached Chicago at 6:30 A.M. and had just one dollar in my pocket — my entire capital.

I went to A. G. Spalding's old store at 108 Madison Street. It was 7:00 A.M. and I wondered why the store was not open, as I had always gone to work when the whistle blew at seven o'clock. I sat on the curb until eight o'clock, when the store opened. I told the clerks who I was, where I was from, and showed them my telegram from Cap Anson. That was my passport.

About ten o'clock Dalrymple, the left-fielder of the Chicago Club and champion batter of the National League, strolled in. Soon others came. I was introduced to them. My hair was long, and I sure looked like the hayseed that I was, compared to those well-groomed men, members of that famous old team.

Finally, Cap Anson came in and spoke to me. He said, "Billy, they tell me that you can run some. Fred Pfeffer is our crack runner. How about putting on a little race this morning?"

I answered that it would be all right with me, and so we all went to the ball park on the lake front, located on Michigan Avenue from Randolph Street to Adams Street. Larry Cochrane, one of our pitchers, loaned me his uniform. Pfeffer came out and he had on running shoes and I had none, so I ran him barefooted, and I'm glad to be able to say that I ran rings around him, beating him by fifteen feet.

You can imagine how the boys razzed Fred for letting a raw country boy beat him. Winning that race opened the hearts of the players to me at once, and I'll always be thankful to Cap for giving me that chance to show off to the best advantage.

As we were leaving the ball park after practice that morning, Cap asked me, "Have you any money?"

I said, "Yeh, I have a dollar."

He said, "Oh, h——l," and handed me a twenty-dollar gold piece.

That act would have endeared him to me for life had he done nothing else to help me, but he was always kind and good to me.

In my freshman years of playing everybody tried to knock the cover off the ball. We knew nothing about bunting or place-hitting that we hear so much about today, and which I think is nine-tenths "hooey" and "apple sauce." When a man walks up to the plate and hits that old pill, he doesn't know where it will go. A round ball coming toward you with terrific speed, or an in or out curve, or a drop, trying to hit that ball with a round bat the odds are seventy-five to one that you will slice it instead of hitting it squarely on the nose.

Therefore the weakness of nine players out of ten is batting. It takes years to make a real slugger out of most men. Very few men are good batters, good fielders and base runners. Most men excel in one feature — you can't get all the possums up one tree.

My weakness was batting. I had never faced a trained, experienced pitcher. I would work all week, and when we played it would be a Saturday afternoon.

The first major-league pitcher I ever faced was Long Jim Whitney, of the Bostons. He had speed to burn, like John Clarkson and "Old Hoss" Radbourne, of the famous Providence team. He pitched and won twenty games in succession. If my memory serves me, he pitched fifty-six games one season.

I struck out the first four or five times at bat. The ball would pass me and be on its way back to the pitcher before I swung at it. I corrected this defect by using a lighter bat and not gripping it clear to the end. Being a left-handed batter, I grasped my right hand at the end of the bat and my left hand about three or four inches farther up on my bat, and in that way I could hit quicker. Then, I used to pull away from the ball; instead of stepping straight ahead with my right foot, I stepped away from the plate. The pitcher would keep the ball on the farther side of the plate and I'd miss the old apple. Mike Kelly showed me how to do it, and I soon caught on. One season I batted .356 and was fourteenth in the list. Cap Anson led the league that year with a batting average of .428. I am drawing on my memory for these figures, as I haven't seen a Yearbook for thirty years. I bat left-handed and throw right-handed.

In my day the pitcher's box was only forty-five feet away from the home plate — today it is sixty feet — and we had a dead ball, not the "rabbit ball" they have been using. Move the pitchers up to forty-five feet and see if the sluggers of today will be putting them over the fence as often as they do now — and I am not underestimating the ability of any of the boys at any stage of the game.

I trained myself to bunt and was the first who ever tried that style of reaching first base. The first time I tried it was against Radbourne. He came in leisurely after the ball and when he got his hands on the sphere I was over first base. He didn't throw the ball to first, just stood there and looked, then laughed and walked over to first and shook my hand, and said:

"That's a new one on me, and you're the fastest man on your feet I have ever seen." That was when I "clicked," as they say on Broadway, when some actor or actress from the sticks knocks 'em cold.

I could run a hundred yards in ten seconds, and was the first to circle the baseball diamond in fourteen seconds from a standing start, touching all bases. I don't know that it has ever been beaten. I do not see how human legs can work any faster. I am not tooting my horn to sell you any clams, but I could steal the bases and play the outfield as well as any of 'em in my day. My speed would enable me to catch many fly balls that other fielders would not even attempt to get.

～ The National Game ～

I believe that one great weakness in baseball today is base-running. There is nothing which gets the nerve of an opposing team, especially the pitcher and catcher, as to see a fellow running wild on the bases; and it thrills the crowds, too, and brings the grand stand and bleachers to their feet.

One season when I played with the Chicago National League team we were leading the league, but we struck a losing streak because some of the boys were breaking the rules. A. G. Spalding and Cap Anson hired Billy Pinkerton to check up on the bunch. He "tailed" us for two weeks and handed A. G. his report. We received notice one day after the game that he wanted to see all the members of the team in the clubhouse after practice the next morning. The gang were all on edge and speculated on what was in the air. They went through their practice with as much vim and ginger as though they were in a real game. We all lined up. Spalding began by complimenting us as a team, saying no club in the league had anything on us, and that we could play rings around any of them, but that we were surely on the toboggan slide and unless we braced up we would lose the championship.

Spalding said, "I know the cause of this slump." Then he sprang Billy Pinkerton's report, which told where every man had been, who were his companions, and when he went to bed. Then he asked, "What will I do?"

Mike Kelly jumped up and said, "Soak us fifty plunks each; and don't worry, A. G., we'll bring home the rag at the end of the season." And we did. We won the championship, but it was the hardest fight we ever had, and few teams ever have had to fight harder up to the last day in order to win the flag.

— The Power of Prayer —

We closed the season away from home, winding up the season in Boston. We were neck and neck with the Giants. That was the season they were given the famous name "Giants." Jim Murtrie, their manager, sat on the bench watching them winning an uphill game, and he said: "Look at them! They're giants, every one of 'em!" And they are known around the world today as the "Giants."

We had four games to play; New York had three games to play with Philadelphia and a postponed game, making four also. On the last day we were one game ahead of New York; we had one game to play and New York had one double-header; if we lost our game and the Giants won both their games, we were sunk.

We were all nervous and serious; we had promised Spalding we would "bring home the bacon."

The last game was played on Thursday. I used to speak on Sundays when on trips — we never played on Sundays those days — and the Young Men's Christian Association would arrange a schedule for me to speak. On Wednesday nights I used to go to prayer meetings.

"Silver" Flint, our old catcher, came to me that Wednesday evening after supper and said: "Billy, are you going to prayer meeting tonight?"

I said, "Yes."

He replied, "I guess I'll go with you, but don't tell the gang."

So off we went, and if I remember correctly it was to the Park Congregational Church, known as "brimstone corner," over on Tremont Street.

On our way over he said, "Billy, I ain't prayed much for years, but I was taught to pray. Do you believe God will help us win that game tomorrow, and help New York to lose one?"

I said, "Sure, the Lord will; and you and I, Frank, will do the praying for the whole team."

Frank said, "Billy, I don't know what to do in a prayer meeting, haven't been in one for years. I would know what to do in a poker game."

I replied, "You just sit still and pray silently."

We prayed on our way there, while there, and on our way back to the old United States Hotel, where we were "parked."

Well, sir, the next day Boston sent Radbourne against us. He had beaten the tar out of us the opening game. We went after Rad hammer and tongs. I led off with a two-bagger against the right-field fence. Kelly and Gore followed with hits, and Cap Anson knocked the cover off. We had three runs over the plate quicker than you could say "scat!" We soon sent Old Hoss Radbourne to the showers, and we won the game.

Ferguson, of the Phillies, pitched and won both games against New York, and we went home "champs."

You ask me how much did the prayers have to do with winning that game and the Giants losing two? Well, I believe the Lord helped us win that game, and shall always believe so unless He tells me differently when I get to heaven.

Our reception on arrival in dear old Chicago was equal to Napoleon's on his victorious return to Paris. Spalding had a banquet for us at the Palmer House. He remitted the fines he assessed after Billy Pinkerton's report.

In those days the ball players had free access to all the theaters, and the actors and actresses also had the same privileges to the grand stand. There was a mighty strong tie of affection between the professions.

Tom Keene, the famous tragedian, who starred in Shakespearean plays, such as *Richard III, Hamlet, Merchant of Venice*, wanted me to travel with him as an understudy. He came to see me in New York, when the Giants played on Staten Island, and urged me to accept his offer, but I refused. I know I chose wisely when I said "No," although at that time I had no idea of becoming an evangelist.

— An Actor's Tribute —

Nat Goodwin was playing in Hooley's Theater in Chicago on our return, and he had a silver ball made, standard size, with solid-gold stitches. We were all guests at Hooley's one night and Nat presented this ball to the club. It had engraved on it "Champions National League."

We all met in Spalding's store the next day to decide what disposition to make of the silver ball. Most of the boys were in favor of presenting it to Cap Anson, but Kelly said, "No: it was given to the club; let's throw dice for it."

So we voted "throw dice." Cap said, "Kell, you suggested throw dice, so you lead off; we won't follow the batting order, or Billy would lead." Kelly threw and chalked up 38. I was the last one to throw. I had never thrown dice before and never have since. Kelly had the ball won until my turn, and I threw 42. Kelly offered me one hundred dollars for the ball, but I refused. I have that ball yet; and every time I look at it, I become young again, and the faces of the old team pass in panorama before my eyes, and the scenes of other days flit by like a butterfly. The great umpire of the Universe has called most of them "out!"

Dalrymple, Gore, Pfeffer, Goldsmith and I are still playing the game of life, waiting to hear the umpire say, "You're out!"

I have my old uniform and my old spiked shoes put away in moth balls. I look at 'em and fondle them as though they were the crown jewels of Egypt. They seem to say, "Hello, Bill! Put us on once more and we'll go out and do our stuff and show some of these birds we are not all in yet." I smile — the old urge is there, as in the days of the long ago; but the "dogs" are a trifle stiff; still I'll wager I can do a hundred yards in fourteen or fifteen seconds now, with a little practice and limbering up.

I walked down State Street in Chicago one Sunday afternoon about forty years ago with some baseball players whose names were world-renowned. We entered a saloon and drank, and then walked to the corner of State and Van Buren streets, which was then a vacant lot and where afterward Siegel & Cooper's big department store was erected.

I never pass that spot to this day that I do not stop, take off my hat, bow my head, and thank God for saving and keeping me. I was passing that corner one day at the noon hour as hundreds of people were pouring out of the stores and office buildings for lunch. I stepped to the edge of the sidewalk, removed my hat and bowed my head. A policeman came up and asked, "Pardner, are you sick? I saw you step to the edge of the sidewalk and remove your hat. If you are I'll call the wagon."

"No, my name is Billy Sunday. I was converted on this lot nearly forty years ago and I never pass here that I do not stop and pray and thank God for saving me. I was praying — that's why I removed my hat."

The policeman removed his cap, and stretching out his hand he said, "Put her there, Bill. I know who you are; you stay and pray as long as you want to and I'll keep the gang away from you."

As we came to the corner of State and Van Buren streets some men and women were in a Gospel wagon, playing instruments and singing Gospel hymns that I heard my mother sing in the log cabin out in Iowa. We sat on the curbstone and listened. A man arose. His name was Harry

Monroe, an ex-gambler and "shover of the queer"—that is, he passed counterfeit money for a gang of counterfeiters. He became converted and was for twenty-five years superintendent of the old Pacific Garden Mission, 100 East Van Buren Street, Chicago, which was established by Colonel George Clark fifty-five years ago, and there has not been a night in all these years that someone has not accepted Christ as Saviour in that mission.

— Joining the Church —

I went to Chicago for a campaign of two months' duration in the spring of 1918 when Germany was making preparations for her famous drive on the Allied lines. The world was excited. Thousands of parents in Chicago had boys overseas for whom they were praying. Our son George was a lieutenant in the Signal Service and was ordered overseas. We had bidden him good-by, perhaps forever. Hearts were heavy, and all Chicago turned their feet toward the tabernacle to hear something in sermon or song that would lift the burden and bring surcease from sorrow.

The tabernacle was built on the north side of the city where the Drake Hotel and those great apartment houses now stand. I said to the people of Chicago, "Whatever amount you give me for a free-will offering at the close of my campaign here, I will give to the old Pacific Garden Mission where I found Jesus as my Saviour." They gave me sixty-three thousand dollars, and I gave every cent to the mission, and with that amount they purchased the building on South State Street where they are now located.

Well, we sat on the curb listening to men and women playing on cornets and trombones and singing Gospel hymns that many of the churches have blue-penciled as being too crude for these so-called enlightened days; but these hymns stir memories that drive folks back to their mother's God and Christ, and, compared with this, semijazz, rattletrap, dishwater music is as useless as a glass eye at a keyhole and will never make a dent in your sin-covered heart.

Harry Monroe stepped out and said, "Don't you men want to hear the story of men who used to be dips (pickpockets), yeggs (safe-blowers), burglars, second-story workers, drunkards, and have done time in the big house, and who today are sober, honest, have good homes, and are trusted and respected; of women who used to sell their womanhood to whoever would buy, were slaves to dope and drink, and are now married and have children of their own? Come down to the mission and hear stories of redeemed lives that will stir you, no matter whether you have ever been inside of a church or have wandered away from God and decency."

I turned to the crowd that sat there with me, and said, "Boys, I bid the old life good-by." Some laughed, some smiled, some shrugged their shoulders, and some looked with mingled expressions of admiration and disgust. One fellow said, "All right, Billy, if that's the way you feel about it."

I went to the mission that evening and liked what I heard. I went back again and again, and one night I went forward and publicly accepted Christ as my Saviour. If the same floor is in that old building I can show you the knot hole in the board upon which I knelt that dark and stormy night forty years ago. I have followed Jesus from that day to this every second, like the hound on the trail of the fox, and will continue until he leads me through the pearly gate into the presence of God and it closes on its jeweled hinges.

I went over to the West Side of Chicago and joined the Jefferson Park Presbyterian Church. I afterward became an elder and superintendent of the Sunday school of that church of which Dr. Frank DeWitt Talmage was pastor, the son of the famous T. DeWitt Talmage. Some years later, in 1903, I was ordained by the Chicago Presbytery, of which I am still a member. The day I was ordained I lost twenty pounds. My knees trembled as badly as old Belshazzar's must have done when God wrote his funeral notice on the wall of the banquet hall in Babylon. Dr. J. G. K. McClure, president of Lake Forest, was the moderator. He appointed Professor Enos, of McCormick Theological Seminary, to examine me on church history, and when the professor asked me about St. Augustine, I replied, "He didn't play in the National League, I don't know him." So I muffed the first ball he threw at me. I tried to steal second, but they caught me between bases. The umpire, Dr. Herrick Johnson, then said, "Mr. Moderator, I move you this needless examination stop. What difference does it make if he knows about Alexander, Savonarola and Cleopatra, or 'Pop' Anson? God has used him to win more souls to Christ than all of us combined, and must have ordained him long before we even thought of it. I move you that he be admitted to the Presbytery and we give him the right hand of fellowship and the authority of the Presbyterian Church." When Doctor Johnson said that I threw my arms around him for helping me reach home.

The reason I joined Jefferson Park Presbyterian Church was that I had a sweetie in that church, named Helen A. Thompson, and her name has been Helen A. Sunday since the fifth day of September, 1888.

For three nights after my acceptance of Christ as Saviour I never slept a wink. I was afraid of the horse laugh the boys would give me when we showed up for practice on Wednesday morning and for the game Wednesday afternoon. In those days we did not play ball every day and never on Sunday. I shall never forget, when I entered the grounds that morning with fear and trembling, I said to myself, "I am not a thief, I am not a drunkard. Why should I worry?"

The first man to meet me and grab my hand was Mike Kelly, one of the best all-around ball players that ever wore a uniform. He could play any position, was a great batter and a peach of a base runner. He said, "Billy, I see by the papers what you have done. Religion ain't my long suit, and I haven't been to mass for so long I have forgotten how the priest looks." Mike was a Catholic. He then went on to say, "I won't knock you, my boy, and if anyone knocks you I will knock them." Up rushed Pop Anson, the captain, and the greatest batter year in and year out that ever swung a bat. Then the entire team — Clarkson, Flint, Williamson, Gore, Burns, Dalrymple and the rest of the boys — all glad-handed me and patted me on the back. I felt as if a millstone had been dropped from my shoulders.

⸺ The Power of Prayer ⸺

That afternoon we were playing the old Detroit team composed of some great players — Brouthers, Dunlap, Richardson, White, Rowe, Hanlon, Thompson and Bennett. Oh, boy, how that crowd could hit! Later on when I was with Pittsburgh we were playing this same Detroit bunch and we had them beat 9 to 0 in the last half of the ninth inning. They had two men out and then started to hit. They pounded out singles, doubles, triples and home runs, and before I could get my hands on a long fly to deep right center for the third out, they had pushed ten runs over the plate and beat us 10 to 9. That's a sample of how they could hit the pill.

Well, on this famous afternoon in Chicago, the first game I played afer I became a Christian, we had them beat three to two in the last half of the ninth inning. They had two out, a man on second and a man on third. Charlie Bennett, their old catcher, was at bat and had two strikes and three balls on him. He could not hit a high ball close to his body, but he could kill a low ball.

John Clarkson was pitching for us. I believe John was the king of all pitchers of all time. He was about six feet tall, weighed one hundred and eighty pounds, and had the best pair of shoulders I have ever seen for a pitcher. They were abnormally large and extremely slanting or drooping; he could never get a ready-made suit of clothes that would fit him.

He threw a zipper ball with terrific speed; it would dip down and then shoot up as it reached the batter, an exceedingly hard ball to hit. Bennett was a right-handed batter but always would swing late at the ball and nine times out of ten he would hit to right center field. I was playing right field that day and was playing deep — that is, far back — hoping that if he hit the last one he would knock it over my head.

I called in to John Clarkson, the pitcher, "One more, John, and we've got 'em." John braced himself for one supreme effort, intending to keep the ball high and in close to the batter, but his foot slipped and the ball went low. Charlie hit it square on the nose. The instant the bat cracked against the ball I glanced up and saw it coming out to me and I could tell it was going over my head. I turned and ran with the oncoming ball. I could run one hundred yards in ten seconds flat and was the first man who ever circled the diamond in fourteen seconds from a standing start and touched all the bases. I do not know that it has ever been beaten.

As I ran I offered up a prayer, something like this: "O Lord, I'm in an awful hole, and if you ever help me, please do it now and you haven't much time to make up your mind."

The grand stand and bleachers had overflowed with people and they were standing along the wall in right and left fields. I saw that the ball was going to drop in the edge of the crowd, and I yelled, "Get out of the way," and they opened up like the Red Sea did for the rod of Moses.

I glanced up and saw the ball coming. I leaped into the air and shot out my right hand and the ball hit and stuck fast as my fingers closed over it. I lost my balance and fell but jumped up with the ball in my hand.

I have never seen such tremendous excitement in my life. The crowd leaped out of the grand stand and surged across the field like waves of the sea. They threw cushions, pop bottles and hats into the air. Up rushed Tom Johnson, who was later mayor of Cleveland, Ohio, threw his arms around me and shoved a ten-dollar bill into my hand and said, "Billy, buy yourself a new hat and come to the Palmer House tomorrow and I will buy you the best suit of clothes in Chicago." Tom bought me my first tailor-made suit, for I had been buying mine from mail-order houses.

When we reached the clubhouse the members of my team hugged me and helped to take off my uniform and dress me. The crowd was waiting and they rushed up and took me on their shoulders. There was a dark brown–eyed, black-haired girl named Helen Thompson, now Mrs. Sunday, waiting for me at the gate and she threw her arms around me and kissed me. That was okay — we were engaged.

You may laugh at my prayer and attempt to analyze it by all the rules of logic and theology, but I believe God helped me get that ball that famous day and I shall keep on believing it until I get to heaven and God tells me otherwise, which I know He will not.

The Chicago Ball Club sold Mike Kelly to Boston for ten thousand dollars, an enormous price in those days. Mike said that he would go if they paid him half the purchase money, and so they gave him a check for five thousand dollars. He said to me, "Billy, put your eyeballs on that."

John L. Sullivan was then on the pinnacle of fame. He went around with a subscription paper and in six hours collected seventeen thousand five hundred dollars with which to buy a house, furnish it, and present it to Mike. They had a balance of fifteen hundred dollars which they deposited in a bank to Mike's credit.

At the end of the season Mike had spent the five thousand dollars purchase money, his five-thousand-dollar salary and the fifteen hundred out of the bank, and when he died the Elks Lodge buried him in Mt. Hope Cemetery. Mike had sat with me on the corner of State and Van Buren streets in Chicago that Sunday afternoon forty years ago when I said, "I am through living this way; I am going to Jesus Christ."

A. G. Spalding took two clubs around the world in 1888 to educate other nations in the great American game of baseball. I was the second man he asked to sign a contract to be a member of his team and would have gone on the trip but for an accident in Philadelphia.

— Big Ed Williamson —

While sliding into second base head-first my right knee struck a stone and tore the ligaments loose from my kneecap. I went to Washington and called in Dr. McGruder, who was one of the doctors that cared for President Garfield when he was shot by Guiteau. He said to me, "Billy, if you take that trip and play ball, it's eighty-five to one that you will be a cripple all your life, but if you follow my directions I will have that leg as good as ever in two months."

My knee was swollen as large as my head, but I followed Doctor McGruder's advice and he kept his word, for in less than two months it was as good as ever and it has never bothered me to this day.

Among those who took the trip was Ed Williamson, our shortstop. He was an "Apollo," strong as Dempsey and active as Corbett. He was forty-eight inches around the chest and could throw a ball farther than any man, and I have never heard of anyone beating his record. The boys said that Ed drank too much wine on the trip and weighed about two hundred and forty pounds when he reached home. In crossing the English Channel a terrific storm arose and the captain of the boat said, "I'm afraid she won't make it, put on life preservers." Ed buckled on two, for he didn't think one would float him.

The boat was rolling in the sea, her decks were awash, and she would be on her beam ends. The wind screamed and howled. Almost everybody was praying. Ofttimes men turn to God in their distress and forget him in their prosperity. Ed's wife was kneeling on one side of him and Mrs. Spalding on the other.

Ed cried out, "O Lord, I ain't fit or ready to die, and if this boat goes down I'll be in hell before midnight, and it's nine o'clock now. If you will spare my life I will quit my drinking and gambling and live as I ought to live."

The storm passed, the boat weathered the blast, and the boat landed in England. Ed came back to Chicago and started a saloon and gambling place on Dearborn Street north of Madison. I had quit playing baseball and was assistant secretary of the Y.M.C.A. in Chicago, and had organized a Yoke-fellows band to stand on street corners and go through saloons and gambling houses inviting men to come to the Y.M.C.A. "men-only" meetings.

— The Mighty Fall —

Most of the saloon workers and bartenders and gamblers and faro dealers knew me, for they were all baseball fans, and so I had carte blanche in all the joints. Ed would take me back into his private office, lock the door and cry, and so would I.

I would say, "Ed, why don't you cut it out and get on the water wagon?" He would say, "Billy, I can't. I don't know anything else to do. I am batting fouls and can't get the ball fair." He went to Hot Springs, Arkansas, one of the most health-giving spots on earth, but Ed had waited too long and he died.

Frank Flint, our old catcher, caught for nineteen years, and that was before they had chest protectors, masks, shin guards and gloves. Every bone in his hands had been broken, his nose and ribs broke, and he could not shut his hands, the finger joints were so stiff. He had a few hangouts where he was always sure to be found, and I have often found him in the back rooms of his haunts and given him money to get a bed or something to eat. His wife left him and started a boarding house on Cottage Grove Avenue on the South Side of Chicago.

A paroxysm of coughing seized him, and he leaned over the railing and coughed and coughed. Down the street came a woman, wearing a sealskin coat, storm collar turned about her neck and ears, diamonds in her ears and on her fingers, and showing signs of affluence and ease of other days. The woman was Frank's wife. She took one look at him and the love came back as in the days of old.

She rushed up to the shivering, coughing, bleeding gladiator of the diamond with the blood dripping from his nose and lips, and cried out, "My God, Frank, is that you?" He nodded his head, for he was so weak he could not speak. She summoned a policeman and a carriage and took him to her boarding house, from where she called five of the best doctors in Chicago, including Dr. N. S. Davis, the lung specialist, and Doctor Etheridge, our family doctor.

They took his temperature and put their stethoscopes to his heart and lungs. They watched and nursed him for days, and when a relapse came Doctor Etheridge turned to Mrs. Flint and whispered, "He hasn't long to live. Perhaps he has some last message he wishes to leave. Go and ask him." She said, "Oh, doctor, I can't do it. You ask him." "No," said Doctor Etheridge, "you tell him."

She bit her lips and, bending over him as the tears trickled down her cheeks, said, "Frank, the doctor says you are very sick and it won't be long until the Umpire calls you out." Frank looked up and whispered to Mrs. Flint, "Send for Billy Sunday."

She phoned for me and I hurried to his bedside. I bent low over him and he whispered, "The way I used to live don't give me any comfort now, Bill. I can see myself going up to draw my pay every two weeks. I've gone out to play when I've been so drunk that if a fellow hit a foul fly it would look like two or three balls up in the sky and I would not know which one to try for; and when my turn came to bat I could hardly see the ball coming. I can hear the crowds cheering, but it don't do me any good now. Billy, if I don't reach home and the Umpire calls me out, will you say a few words?"

I promised him that I would and left the house. A few hours later the pupils of his eyes dilated, his muscles became taut, and he threw his gnarled hands to his throat as if to tear it open so that he could breathe easier. He seemed to be trying to stretch a three-bagger into a home run. He rounded third, going hard, and appeared to lunge as though trying to beat the throw in time. The spectators seemed to be sitting on the edge of their seats, pulling hard for Frank to win. The Umpire leaned over the prostrate form and shouted, "You're out!" and poor old Frank went to the clubhouse.

The funeral services were conducted by an Episcopal rector, and I preached the sermon. Around his coffin stood bankers from La Salle Street, men and women from the sporting world, actors and actresses. In my stumbling and tearful baseball jargon I tried to tell them to play the game of life fairly, to make sacrifice hits, keep out of the error column, touch all the bases and reach home with the winning run.

Since that Sunday afternoon sitting on the curbstone on the corner of State and Van Buren streets, I have preached to more than eighty millions of people who have looked into my face, to millions through the press and over the air, and will keep on until God says, "It is enough, come up higher."

⏤ In Y.M.C.A. Work ⏤

I quit playing ball when I was a top-notcher and went into Y.M.C.A. work in Chicago. L. W. Messer, general secretary of the Y.M.C.A., was the first general secretary to conceive the idea of dividing the work into departments. He appointed me secretary of the religious department. Walter Wood, now head of the Philadelphia Y.M.C.A., was appointed director of the educational work, thus I held the honor of being the first religious-work director in the Y.M.C.A. in the United States.

I was drawing a big salary for those days in baseball, and accepted a position that paid me only one thousand dollars a year—eighty-three dollars a month. I worked six days a week until ten o'clock at night. I was offered two thousand dollars a month by J. Palmer O'Neil, president of the Pittsburgh Pirates, to come back for the three remaining months of the season; but I refused, and worked on, walking to work and back every day, going without lunch because I couldn't spare the money, with wife and two children. Helen and George were little tots. Nobody called me a grafter then, and I'd advise them not to do so now unless they want to take a ride in the Red Cross wagon.

I used to spend some of my winters firing for the Chicago & North Western Railway. I thought I might become an engineer after I quit playing baseball.

I also spent several winters at Northwestern University at Evanston, Illinois, studying and coaching the football and baseball teams.

While attending college at Evanston, I roomed in the home of a lady named Mrs. Wilder. She lived next door to Frances E. Willard, president of the National W.C.T.U. Miss Willard was writing her autobiography, Mrs. Wilder was assisting and correcting the manuscript and she allowed me to read some of it. I remember one gem, which I consider one of the most beautiful ever written; it has been one of my guiding stars. It is this:

We have all cast anchor for a little while beside this island of a world. We are all bound for the Continent of Immortality. Our sails are all spread, and we must soon leave the harbor for the open sea. Let us take on board a cargo which will be worth something in that land where we are to spend so long a time.

The first team that ever went into the South for spring training was the Chicago club. We went to Hot Springs, Arkansas, and took the baths in the famous water; and to this day I do not believe there is a spot that can surpass it for training athletes. Now all the clubs follow the lead of old Chicago, and they spend millions of dollars getting the boys in shape.

I remember one spring Jim McCormick, one of our pitchers, reported looking like a tub. He couldn't get into shape to leave when the club started on their barnstorming tour, so Cap Anson left me behind to watch Jim and make sure he took his exercise and baths. When Jim was going right he was a hard man to hit. He had a side-arm, underhand ball, with a slight upward shoot; if you hit it, you'd drive it up in the air. He soon passed his usefulness and was living in Paterson, New Jersey, when I was there conducting a series of meetings. He was very sick and Mrs. Sunday and I would often go to see him. He always expected and we never failed to leave him a bill. He died a few months later.

— Off the Diamond —

People used to idolize ball players and follow them around like a dog with his master. They hung around the hotels just to catch a glimpse of their favorite.

The ball players today save their money, while in the olden days "easy come, easy go" was the rule, although many are well fixed in their old age, and have become noted.

John Ward, captain of the Giants, became attorney for the Brooklyn Rapid Transit Co.

John K. Tener, who used to pitch for Chicago, became governor of Pennsylvania, and gave old, brokendown ball players jobs as guards at the penitentiary.

Ad Gumbert, Chicago pitcher, became sheriff of Allegheny County, Pennsylvania, of which Pittsburgh is the county seat.

Ed Swartwood was deputy sheriff under Gumbert.

"Home Run" Frank Baker owns several farms on the Eastern Shore of Maryland.

Cy Young lives on his big farm near Canton, Ohio.

Fred Clark owns 1500 acres near Winfield, Kansas.

Fred Dunlap became a diamond merchant. He would buy diamonds from fellows who were hard up, then sell them for a big profit. He was an expert in judging their value. He could tell within five dollars what Bailey, Banks & Biddle, of Philadelphia, or Tiffany's, of New York, would give. Fred could neither read nor write. I used to write his letters for him. A woman in Detroit got sweet on Fred and would write him. I read the letters to him, but balked on answering them after I found out that she was married. When we played in Detroit, and he would go to bat, a boy would dash out with a horseshoe made of flowers higher than Fred's head. At that time I had not heard the advice:

> Do right — and fear no man;
> Do not write, and fear no woman.

When I joined the old White Sox, in 1883, the ball grounds were located on the lake front at the foot of Randolph, Washington and Madison streets, near where the Art Institute now stands. Later they were moved to the west side of the city, and in going from the grounds I always went north on Throop Street to the hotel where I boarded.

On the corner of Throop and Adams streets stood Jefferson Park Presbyterian Church. One Sunday evening I went there to attend Christian Endeavor meeting, and was introduced to a black-eyed, black-haired young lady eighteen years old, named Helen Amelia Thompson. Her father was William Thompson, who at that time had the largest milk dairy and ice-cream establishment in the city. The family lived across the street from the church.

The first time I saw those flashing black eyes and dark hair and white teeth, I said to myself, "There's a swell girl." I always planned to attend that church and the young people's meetings whenever our club was playing in Chicago.

After several weeks I braced up one evening and asked Miss Thompson if I could see her home. She shied off for a minute, then smiled and said, "Yes," and from that time on I was hooked.

I used to attend prayer meeting and always sat on a row of seats along the wall where I could keep one eye on Nell, as everybody called her, and the other on the preacher. She had a fellow and tried to "team me up" with a girl chum of hers, but I didn't like the other girl. She had a camel-like neck and humped over when she walked, liquid gazelle-like eyes, was flat-footed and had a drawling, croony voice like Rudy Vallee's, and I passed her up as a pay car does a tramp.

I passed the Thompson home on my way to practice at ten o'clock in the morning, back to lunch at noon, back for the game in the afternoon, then home for supper. Nell used to time my goings and comings and would be out sweeping the front steps and the sidewalk. If we had an extra-long game, she swept on until I showed up. I would explain the game, who won or lost, how many hits and runs I made.

~ **Wedding Bells** ~

Finally, one time I went to see her — it was New Year's night, 1888. She had on an ox-blood cashmere dress, and a natural-colored lynx neckpiece thrown about her shoulders, which her parents had given her for Christmas, and which I had never seen before. Oh, boy! She was a knock-out! She looked like I imagine the Queen of Sheba did when she visited Solomon. She had ditched her beau, and I had given the gate to a girl I had out in Iowa. So I braced right up, just before midnight, and asked "Nell, will you marry me?" She came back at me so quick it almost floored me: "Yes, with all my heart."

I went home feeling as though I had wings on my feet. I didn't sleep that night. Visions of those black eyes stared at me from the darkness and turned night into day.

That spring I was sold to Pittsburgh; it was optional with me whether I went or not. A. G. Spalding and Cap Anson said, "Now, Billy, you can stay if you want to, but Pittsburgh will pay you a big increase in salary." So Nell and I talked it over and we decided it would be a good move for me to go, and I did. I had seven hundred dollars saved, and during that season up to the day we were married I saved twelve hundred dollars and sent it all to Nell to bank, and from then until now she has been my banker, bookkeeper and pays all bills.

We have the old sofa in our home on which we used to "spark" and build our castles in the air, many of which have been crushed and lie in ruins at our feet, and some of which still stand, buttressed about by a love that blazes as brightly as it did when we plighted our eternal allegiance forty-three years ago.

I left the team in Indianapolis that evening after the game, and went to Chicago. We were married on September 5, 1988, by Dr. David C. Marquis, of McCormick Theological Seminary, of Chicago, at two o'clock in the afternoon. A. G. Spalding had a box draped for us at the ball grounds and had us come down there before we left for Pittsburgh. The grand stand and bleachers arose and cheered us, and my old teammates of the Chicagos all lined up in front of our box, and with hats off wished us happiness and long life. We left Chicago for Pittsburgh on the Pennsylvania Limited at five o'clock. That same train still runs with the same number—old No. 2. Every time it passes through our home town, Winona Lake, Indiana, ma and I say, "There goes our honeymoon train."

Players could take their wives with them on the swing around the circuit if they wished, but as salaries were not so big and the trips were expensive, they did not often do so. Mrs. Sunday's parents were well-to-do for those days and paid her expenses so she was with me half the season.

When her father heard we were engaged, he "shelled the woods," declaring no daughter of his should ever marry a ball player; but her mother, one of the noblest souls that ever breathed, was on our side, and of course "dad" had to surrender, which he did in July, and Nell wired me in Philadelphia: "Dad says it's all right." That afternoon I made three hits and had five put-outs.

Mrs. Sunday's father became my most loyal supporter, both as a ball player and as an evangelist. I played ball nearly four years after we were married. After I became an evangelist he always came to hear me preach. I suppose the fact that he was an old soldier, member of the 51st Illinois, and was severely wounded in the battle of Shiloh, and that my own father was a member of the 23d Iowa, helped to establish a bond of sympathy; and then I was married to his favorite daughter, Nell. He joined Jefferson Park Presbyterian Church and was "mustered out" a Christian.

Mrs. Sunday and I had no honeymoon in the generally accepted version of taking a vacation or a long trip or a hide-out in some secluded spot. The next day after our wedding I played baseball in Pittsburgh, and when I came to bat—I was the lead-off man, first in the batting order—I was presented with a bronze clock, which sits on the mantel in our home today; also an ice-cream set of a dozen Dresden-china dishes, and a dozen solid-silver spoons in a beautiful silk-lined case. That has been more than forty years ago and we still have the spoons and dishes.

I think one of the greatest threatened dangers to this republic and human life is the danger growing out of the crumbling foundations of the home life.

There is recorded in the faces and burned-out souls of young men and young women enough to stagger us. We are lowering our standards to be in tune with the demands of the devil, instead of the high ideals of God.

The modern dances are disgusting with their brazen pandering to lust. There seems to be but one idea prevalent. We need to get back to the old-time modesty in our dress. I don't mean dress like our grandmothers, with hoop skirts which covered a great deal of territory without touching the subject. Hang up before me the fashion plates of any age, and I will tell you the morals of that age. I think these bathing-beauty contests are an insult to womanhood and a disgrace to the age in which we live.

If we go on exploiting sex in books, in magazines, in the movies, and on the stage, what of the future and of our civilization, of our homes and of the nation?

— Women through the Ages —

There is nothing the matter with the stage or the movies or the talkies that cannot be removed by having clean plays and pictures. Imagine Edwin Booth, Joe Jefferson or Tom Keene or Lawrence Barrett in the slime of the sex-sewage play. The theater can build up, not drag down; it can refine, not sensualize; it can make ladies, not prostitutes; it can make gentlemen, not sheiks. The gulls and the buzzards that feed on offal and the carcasses of the dead have not been more greedy for such carrion than the public has been for sex offal.

No nation can endure with a low standard of womanhood.

History speaks with no uncertain sound of the power of woman to command the admiration and mold the character of the age in which she lives. She has swayed the policy of nations and changed the maps of the world; she is the most powerful factor in the changing story of humanity. It's not the king on the throne or the President in the White House, or the statesman with his logic and eloquence, or the soldier with his blood-stained laurels of military glory who controls this world—it's woman.

Women seem to be favorites with the Lord from the order of creation. God created Adam, then Eve. She is an improved edition over man. No-where in the Bible can you find where God ever told a woman to love—He knew she would without a command. If you search the dust-covered pages of history you will find that in all ages and countries women have been loved and hated, adored and disgraced, honored and dishonored. Man has been her brutal tyrant and her slave. The mother who allows a young girl to joy ride until the roosters crow, opens the front door and invites sorrow and disgrace to become a guest in her home. When booze and virtue take a joy ride, virtue never comes back home.

Many parents imagine their children haven't "arrived" socially unless they can drink and roll their own. Sons and daughters brought up in idle-ness and untrained in the expenditure of money rapidly acquire profligate habits and figure in the disgraceful escapades that scandalize society.

The general moral corruption of society, the sin in official and family life, will bring America to ruin as sure as God sits on His throne. The foundations are rotting, they are being eaten away, the canker worms of

sinful practices are gnawing at our hearts. The whole structure will top-
ple and fall if the fundamental laws underlying the home and nation are
ignored.

I continued to play ball for four years before I became a Christian. I
had an inborn respect and admiration for a preacher and the church. I
inherited it from my father and mother. Mother told me that my father
was a Lutheran. Grandfather used to have periodical spells of several
months apart when he drank liquor, but never bought the liquor himself;
he would get it from the bootleggers. You see, I began to hate booze in my
youth, and as the years come and go my hatred for the cursed business
and the bootlegger increases. It was the same back in those early days —
the bootlegger was the scourge of society; and it takes two to make a bootlegger — the fellow who sells the stuff and the one who buys it.

I never drank much. I was never drunk but four times in my life. I never
drank whisky or beer; I never liked either. I drank wine, and I like wine
now, but I have not drunk whisky, beer or wine since I was converted
forty years ago. I used to go to the saloons with the baseball players, and
while they would drink highballs and gin fizzes and beer, I would take
lemonade or sarsaparilla.

I would see ball players blast earth like meteors for a year or two, drink
and dissipate, then drop by the wayside and become bums or bartenders,
or runners for gambling dens; and when a man became thirty or thirty-
five years old his joints would stiffen or his eyes would dim and he was
not qualifying for any position in business, and whatever he did he would
have to start from the bottom.

⌐ The Demon Rum ⌐

I said to myself, as I checked up and took an inventory of my conduct,
"If I keep on and live this way and do what they do just to retain their

friendship and show them I am no milksop, I will soon join the 'has-beens,' take down the sign 'is' and hang up the 'was,' and the future will hold nothing for me but the memory of what might have been." I said, "I have only one life to live, and I don't want to muff that."

I am the sworn, eternal and uncompromising enemy of the liquor traffic and have been for thirty-five years. I saw that nine-tenths of the misery, poverty, wrecked homes and blighted lives were caused by booze. I saw it rob men of their manhood and clothe them in rags, take away their health, rob their families, incite the father to butcher his wife and child, rip the shirt off the back of a shivering man, take the last drop of milk from the breast of a nursing mother, send women to steaming over a washtub to manicure their finger nails to the quick to get money to feed a hungry brood, while it sent their father home from their hell holes, a bleary-eyed, bloated face, staggering, reeling, jabbering wreck while all hell screamed with delight and heaven wept and the angels hid behind their harps. I drew my sword and have never sheathed it, and never will as long as there is a distillery or brewery or a bootlegger or speak-easy on earth. I put twelve states dry before we voted on the Eighteenth Amendment.

The real reason for the Federal Prohibition Amendment is that the wet minority has never respected the law and has never allowed the dry majority to be dry.

The liquor traffic always has been criminal and lawless, caring nothing for human well-being, fighting for its own privilege to exploit the people.

I challenge the enemies of Prohibition to show me a city on earth where the sale of liquor has been a benefit, morally, spiritually, commercially or financially.

I had a three-year contract with the Philadelphia club of the National League which expired in 1894. At the close of the first season in Phila-delphia I felt I should give up ball playing. I had worked and studied the Bible in the Chicago Y.M.C.A. during one or two winters and I was being urged to accept a position there, so I asked for my release, but was promptly refused. I continued to work and study all that winter in the Y.M.C.A., receiving no pay whatever, fully expecting to go back to Philadelphia to play ball. I knew it wouldn't be right for me to jump my contract in order to go into Christian work.

— A Difficult Decision —

In the spring of 1892 Mr. Baker, then president of the Philadelphia club, ordered me to report and go south with the club for spring training. I told him I would report April first in shape to play that day if necessary. I always took excellent care of myself. I used to coach the baseball club of Northwestern University and go to school there in the winter, and previous to that I had fired for the Chicago & North Western Railway in the winter.

I was greatly troubled. I felt I was called definitely to enter Christian work, and yet the way was blocked, so I made it a matter of most earnest prayer and even went so far as to make a proposition, saying, "Lord, if I don't get my release by March twenty-fifth, I will take that as assurance you want me to continue to play ball; if I get it before that date I will accept that as evidence you want me to quit playing ball and go into Christian work."

On March seventeenth, St. Patrick's Day, I was notified by Nick Young, then president of the National League, that I could have my release if I wanted it. I wired, "I do; send it."

The day I received my release I was speaking at the noon meeting in Farwell Hall. When the meeting closed, up came Jim Hart, then president of the Chicago baseball club, saying that the Cincinnati club had authorized him to offer me a contract for $5000 for the season. Gosh, I didn't know what to do.

Five thousand berries looked as big as the Empire State Building in New York does to a rube from the sticks, but there was the promise I had made the Lord. I didn't eat for two days and I couldn't sleep. I saw $5000 everywhere I looked.

I asked friends what to do, among them Cyrus McCormick, then president of the McCormick Harvesting Machine Company, also president of the Y.M.C.A., and J. V. Farwell. About half of those whom I asked said, "Stick to your promise," but others advised me to play ball during the summer and go into the Y.M.C.A. in the fall when the ball season was over. Mrs. Sunday said, "There is nothing to consider; you promised God to quit."

I prayed all night and the next day I refused the Cincinnati offer and went to work in the Y.M.C.A. for $83.33 per month, $1000 a year.

That was in 1892 when a tidal wave of depression struck the country. I used to walk to and from work each day, go without lunch, had my old clothes made over and dyed to look new, and wore a celluloid collar to save laundry. I worked hard and they raised my salary to $1200 the second year and to $1500 the third year.

About this time, Rev. J. Wilbur Chapman was looking for a man as an assistant to put up tents, sell books in his meetings and organize committees and speak in overflow meetings. Peter Bilhorn, a Gospel singer, told him of me. He came to Chicago to see me and talk with me. He offered me the job and I accepted. I felt it would be a big help to me in the future.

I traveled with him two years and a half. We separated for our homes for the holidays, and while we were getting ready for a Christmas celebration for our children, Helen and George, who were little tots then, Doctor Chapman wired me that he had decided to quit evangelistic work and had accepted the pastorate of the Bethany Presbyterian Church in Philadelphia. It was called John Wanamaker's church, as he was superintendent of the Sunday school. While we worried and prayed what to do and discussed if I should go back to play baseball, a letter came from Garner, Iowa, telling me that three churches wanted a meeting and had rented the opera house, and asked me to come as the leader. You bet I wired them I'd be there. We knew it was a direct answer to our prayers.

— My First Campaign —

That was the first campaign of my own I ever conducted. Two hundred and sixty-eight people came forward during the eight days, and before I had finished there I received a letter inviting me to Pawnee City, Nebraska. I went to five towns, one after another, before I went home, and from that day until now I have always had more calls than I could accept. I've seen the day when I had calls from towns on the waiting list five years ahead.

Doctor Chapman taught me to preach and gave me the outlines of some of his old sermons which I gladly accepted as I had only seven sermons when I started and could only stay one week. The ministers would beg me to stay longer. I would "stall" and tell them I had to hurry to the next town, which was true, but they would have allowed me to wait a week longer. The reason I could not stay longer was that I was at the bottom of my sermon barrel.

I have sat up all night reading and studying to get more sermons, and as I did and broadened my knowledge and experience, the larger cities began to invite me, until today I have been in every state in the Union, conducted campaigns in most of the larger cities and preached in every city from Portland, Maine, to Seattle, and from Duluth to New Orleans. I used to put up my own tents and care for them. When a rainstorm would come up in the night I would get up and light a lantern that I kept in my room and go down to loosen the ropes, for the rain contracts canvas and rope and the tent would become like a drumhead and pull the stakes, and down would come the tent.

I have sat up all night watching the tent. In one town where I was holding forth in a tent Ringling's circus came to town. It wasn't long before his tent men came over to look at my tent. They inquired, "Who tied these knots? Who put up this tent?" They congratulated me when I told them that I had.

I learned how from an old circus-tent man, as very few folks knew just how to do it in the towns in which I was working. As ex-President Coolidge once said, "Luck has not much to do with success. Much more depends on being prepared so you can take advantage of luck."

I have worked in towns and received in my free-will offerings scarcely enough to pay my way home. I worked in one whisky-soaked, gambling-cursed, jay-rube town out in the short-grass country on the kerosene circuit for two weeks and had one hundred and twenty-seven people accept Christ as their Saviour. They gave me thirty-three dollars.

When I went to Pawnee City, Nebraska, I was entertained in the home of a hardware merchant named Harrington. An infidel in that section came into his store and was abusing and cursing me and denouncing him for having me as a guest in his home. He said he did not believe in a God, and if there was a God let him strike me dead. He dropped to the floor and before a doctor arrived he was dead. I have seen almost a score of such incidents.

I have never conducted a campaign which I regarded as a failure. Some have a greater degree of success than others. That is usually due to two causes: First, the type of people who live in the town, and second, the cooperation given the meetings by the ministers and the churches. I do not believe there stands a city or town in America that will not turn to

God if the Christian people will present a solid front for God and will work and pray and never dip their colors to the devil.

I started my evangelistic work in opera houses, large churches, or tents, as there were not many buildings suitable in those days. Since the World War, scores, and I dare say hundreds, of cities and towns have built memorial halls and immense auditoriums, and many fraternal organizations and municipalities have erected buildings which are now used for large gatherings. Cities have grown with leaps and bounds and all available property upon which you could build a tabernacle centrally located with parking space for automobiles is occupied with buildings. We had a hard time to find a location in New York. The tabernacle was built at One Hundred and Sixty-eighth Street and Broadway, where the Medical Center now stands.

— Leading the Singing —

The last city in which I conducted a campaign in a tent was Salida, Colorado. I always begin and close a series of meetings on Sunday, and on Saturday night before the closing day in Salida it started to snow. I had ten men with long poles with boards nailed on the end to push and pull the snow from the top of the tent. The snow fell so fast it piled three feet deep on the tent and broke the center poles and the side poles and tore the tent into ribbons. We went into the opera house for the closing services. The mayor ordered out the snow plows to open up the streets and sidewalks. I said then that I would never use a tent again, and I never have.

When I first started in my evangelistic work I tried to lead the singing, although I did not know a note from a horsefly. I knew the song and the tune and supplied the vim, ginger and tabasco sauce.

Later on I picked up some local men, but that proved a flop. Then I looked for a singer and found Fred Fisher, a cousin of Peter Bilhorn, the publisher and Gospel singer. Fred was with me for eleven years. Then I picked up B. D. Ackley as pianist and secretary. He was with me for ten years. He is the author of some of the finest Gospel hymns ever written. Then I found Homer Rodeheaver, who was associated with me for twenty years. The world knows "Rody" so I don't need to spend time eulogizing his wonderful ability.

Now I have Harry Clarke. He possesses most of the highest-grade qualities of all who have gone before and is a coming leader of song.

Many incidents come to my mind. Something happened in almost every city and town that was outstanding. But space forbids that I attempt to recount them all.

One night in Springfield, Illinois, I noticed a big, black-haired, sullen-looking bozo over on my right, glaring at me from under his wrinkled forehead and squinty eyes. His right hand was inside the lapel of his coat. Suddenly he sprang like a tiger, rushed toward the platform from which I was preaching, and drew a rawhide from his coat and lashed me around my legs and body, yelling as he did it, "I have a commission from God to horsewhip you!"

I jumped from the platform and rushed at him with my fist doubled and said, "Well, I have a commission from God to knock the tar out of you, you lobster."

I gave him a solar-plexus and a left hook to the jaw, and by that time five hundred men were tearing down the aisles, and it took the United States marshal, who happened to be in the tabernacle, and eight cops to rescue him. I didn't prosecute him. I have never gone armed.

In the old saloon days the city officials always assigned men to guard me and the house where I stayed, day and night. The plain-clothes men were with me every minute like the Secret Service guards the President.

One of the outstanding moments was in Washington when I was invited by Champ Clark, then Speaker of the House of Representatives, to open a session with prayer. When I finished praying the members broke out into applause and all left their seats to shake my hand. Champ said, "Billy, you will have to leave; we can't call the House to business until you do." Three stenographers took my prayer. The House ordered it printed on special slips and mailed to thousands of their friends. Mr. Ireland, the head stenographer, came to my room to check the prayer to be sure they had it absolutely correct. He said, "We must not make mistakes."

— During the War —

Another outstanding feature was the last day in New York when 7436 people came forward and grasped my hand pledging to accept Christ as their Saviour.

Another was when President Wilson sent for me to come to the White House, and asked me not to go overseas but to stay and help him here at home. He said, "We have speakers and singers and entertainers enough overseas. Not everyone here at home is doing his part like the soldiers are and you have the ears of the people and can go from city to city." I clasped his hand and said, "Mr. President, your wish is law with me." I stayed home and raised one hundred million dollars for Liberty and Victory loans.

— The Christian Life —

I never resort to tricks to hold an audience or set the stage for effect. I have never found an audience a many-headed monster. There is something inherent in the human mind that causes most people to listen with respect to a man preaching the Gospel. We took our character from our forefathers who struck the snow-covered hills of New England with a Bible in one hand and a spelling book in the other, and when they landed at Jamestown they knelt on the open Bible and dedicated this country to God. Someone said that we are three hundred years ahead of South America because the Spaniards went there searching for gold and our ancestors came to this country searching for God.

Christianity creates civilization and the more we apply the principle of Christianity to our lives and business the more civilized we become. It is beyond argument that the highest civilization walks hand in hand with the purest Christianity, and that the man who has the most respect for God's law will have the most respect for man's law, and that the best Christian will make the best citizen.

If you have something interesting and instructive to say and say it with vim, ginger and enthusiasm, an audience will listen. And, believe me, I have had some exciting experiences when individuals have tried to start something!

Every feature considered, I regard Philadelphia and New York as the two most successful campaigns I ever conducted. I have preached to eighty millions of people who have heard my voice, and to millions through the newspapers and over the air who have never seen my face; more than one million have "hit the sawdust trail" to renew their pledges as Christians or to accept Christ as their Saviour.

I estimate I have preached more than 20,000 times; I have spoken on an average of seventy-five times a month. I have preached as often as five times in one day. I did this in Richmond, Virginia, where there were 18,000 people clamoring around the doors unable to get in after I had preached five times.

The first tabernacle was erected in Perry, Iowa. They laid a board floor in that building, and the noise when the people would walk was terrific, so I conceived the idea of using baled shavings or sawdust. In some cities where they have tanneries I used tanbark.

I have never had a stampede or a calamity in a building. A tabernacle is the safest building ever devised in which to handle crowds safely. We always have an army of trained men as ushers, and fifteen to twenty doors. You can push the boards off the side walls, as they are always nailed on the uprights from the outside. I have built about two hundred tabernacles of all sizes, from one of a seating capacity of fifteen hundred to the ones in New York and Chicago that seated 22,000. Chicago built her building three feet longer than New York so they could say that they erected the largest tabernacle ever built in the United States. It was three hundred and three feet long. I have blue prints for the contractor to follow. We can tell within a few hundred feet how much lumber is needed and within half a keg how many nails are needed.

I send a man ahead to oversee the erection of the building, to divide the city into sections for prayer meetings and appoint leaders for each section, and to organize a chorus, taking the church choirs for a nucleus around which to build an organization. We organize a finance committee of the most representative men, with a representative in each church cooperating, and raise enough money to pay half of the current expenses, using that money to pay the lumber and hardware bills and the carpenters. The remaining half we raise in collections. I have never seen a city fail to meet all her financial obligations.

— Playing Ball for the Soldiers —

I was preaching in Los Angeles in September, 1917. Doug Fairbanks and I put on a benefit game for the purpose of buying baseballs, bats, gloves, shoes and masks for the soldiers overseas. A shipload had been sent over and the Germans torpedoed the ship and they all went to Davy Jones' locker. We raised $17,000 in that game.

In Wichita, Kansas, one Sunday morning in the tabernacle when eight thousand people were present, Henry J. Allen, then editor of the Wichita *Beacon*, and one of the most brilliant of a long line of famous editors in that wonderful state of Kansas and afterward governor of that state and also United States Senator, walked upon the platform and asked for the privilege of speaking.

He said, "I have always been a believer in God and in Jesus, but like multitudes of others have not publicly expressed that belief or joined a church, and I here and now before this vast audience do both." Eight thousand people jumped to their feet and cheered.

In Kankakee, Illinois, nearly one hundred business and professional men met and pledged each other that they would all go to the tabernacle, and when I extended the invitation to all who would accept Christ as their Saviours to come forward they would follow the lead of a certain one of their group and all go forward together. That certain man who led that grand march down the sawdust trail was Len Small, three times governor of Illinois and one of my true-blue friends to this day.

In Scranton, Pennsylvania, the business men organized a Christian parade. It was headed by E. M. Rine, then division superintendent of the Delaware, Lackawanna & Western Railroad and now vice president and general manager. Eight thousand men were in line.

⚊ The Graveyard of Evangelists ⚊

I conducted a campaign in Washington in 1918. The tabernacle was built on Government property near the Union Station. The building seated

12,000 people. Almost all the famous statesmen and generals from Europe who came to the United States were brought to the tabernacle and introduced to the audience.

Hon. Josephus Daniels was Secretary of the Navy and one of the outstanding supporters and a constant attendant. One night seated on the platform by me while I preached were Mr. Harding, then senator from Ohio, Champ Clark, then speaker of the House, and Joe Cannon, of Illinois. All three have crossed the river. The memory of that night shines like a star.

When I went to hold a campaign in New York City, there had not been a revival there in forty-one years, not since Moody and Sankey were in the old Hippodrome in 1876.

New York City was known as the "graveyard of the evangelists." It was believed that no evangelist was big enough to touch the heart of Greater New York with its seven million people and its diversified interests.

Newspaper men predicted that my campaign would be a flop.

"The papers will give Sunday a good story for a day or two after he opens, but they'll drop him like a hot potato after a week," they said.

My best friends were unanimous against my going to New York. They agreed that I would be a failure.

The liquor interests said: "We'll pull Billy Sunday's cork in New York." They centered their opposition against me and we felt it in many ways. Many friends advised me that the liquor interests would fight me so hard there that it would be useless to fight back.

Another argument used against my going to New York was that there was no suitable place for a tabernacle in the downtown district or anywhere within convenient reaching distance of it. The only available sight for our tabernacle was away up at 168th Street and Broadway. This is more than ten miles from the heart of New York, or from Brooklyn, Jersey

City, Hoboken or Staten Island, by the Broadway subway. There wasn't an elevated road near it. A surface car ran past the door, but no one rides surface cars in New York except for short distances. They are too slow. The Fifth Avenue bus lines were diverted to reach our tabernacle, but they were slow too. The crowds had to come by the subway, and to get there at night they had to come during the rush hour. If you've never been on a subway train during the rush hour you don't know what it means to pack 'em in like sardines in a box.

To add to the difficulty, the subway where it passed the tabernacle was one hundred and sixteen feet underground. So, to get to the tabernacle from any of the points I have mentioned, they had to fight their way into a subway train in the rush hour, stand packed in for an hour or more, fight to get into an elevator at 168th Street, be lifted one hundred and sixteen feet, then fight to get into the tabernacle. It's a wonder anyone came at all.

All the predictions that people in New York would not listen to the old Gospel came to naught. The people of New York are just like the people of the corn rows out in Iowa or any other place. They are just folks, that's all, with the same hungering for the old-fashioned Gospel of Jesus Christ that I have found everywhere.

When I announced that the services in the tabernacle would begin at seven-thirty o'clock at night, everyone tried to get me to change the hour. But I had too much experience with crowds to change anything.

And my hunch was right. The people would come and did come. They were hungering and thirsting for the Gospel of Jesus Christ and they endured suffering to come and hear it.

Nearly every Saturday night and Sunday night from ten to twenty thousand persons were turned away, so the newspapers said. The newspapers estimated that on the last memorable day sixty thousand were unable to get into the tabernacle.

And the newspapers did print the news of the campaign, printed it by the column and by the page.

I spoke one morning to a bunch of more than a thousand millionaires in the Plaza Hotel, and I gave them the real old Gospel, without any frills, trimming or emasculation. I gave them both barrels and told them where to head in, and when I got through two hundred and twenty-one of them came forward upon my invitation, took my hand and pledged themselves to accept Jesus Christ right there and to live as He wanted.

I spoke all over New York in between my regular meetings in the tabernacle. I spoke to the prisoners in the Tombs, to the missions in the Bowery and elsewhere, to the police and firemen and wherever I had time to go. I sowed the Gospel seed in New York just as a farmer sows down a field with grain.

⏤ The Same Old Ship of Zion ⏤

Some had predicted that I would trim my sermons to suit the New York audience, and many would have liked to have seen me stick on some gold leaf and give the upper works of the old ship a coat of new and more modern paint, but she was still the old Ship of Zion, same captain, same compass, same chart, bound for the same harbor.

I preached in the tabernacle to two million persons. The count was kept by a newspaper man of New York. There were 98,264 trail hitters, more than two army corps to fight the good fight of faith. The count was kept by a Mr. Macavoy, selected for that purpose by the newspapers of New York. When I began to shake the hands of converts Macavoy stood beside me with a mechanical counter, and every time I shook a hand of a person who thus signified that he or she was accepting Christ, Macavoy would register one.

The collections taken during the ten weeks' campaign paid for the tabernacle and all expenses and sixty thousand dollars for conservation work. In addition they gave me $120,485 as my free-will offering, which I turned over in full for overseas work to the Y.M.C.A., Y.W.C.A. and Red Cross.

I am asked, "Have you changed your method or message?" My method is in effect the same, my message is the same in substance. The Gospel never changes. Man's opinion may change, but that does not alter a fact. Styles change, weather changes, your health changes, the war changed the boundaries and governments of the world, the surface of the earth changes—where once there was water, today there is land. We enter the world by birth, we go out by death. Seeds grow under the same conditions as in the beginning. The elements that constitute food and drink will be the basis of nourishment for vegetable, animal and man as long as the world stands.

God has not modernized the methods of creation or changed the stars or planets in their orbits or the ebb and flow of the tide, or given the earth new methods of life or of life development. Your heart is on the left, your liver on the right, and your feet at the end of your legs. And God is the same and His plan of salvation is the same yesterday, today and forever.

Religion draws people the same today, but the hard, fast materialism and liberalism that have gripped the world make it difficult to induce them to accept Christ. It requires as much effort today to get a boy fifteen years old as it did twenty years ago to get a man fifty years of age to turn from sin.

⁓ Flagging Zeal ⁓

The liberalistic heresy has almost stifled Christianity. Fifty thousand churches recently failed to obtain one convert during the year. It is estimated that nine thousand churches throughout this country have closed their doors or reported "vacant," "inactive."

In Pentacostal days "three thousand" were added to the church in one day. A few days later, five thousand men, and a few days later, multitudes of both men and women. How large was the church? One hundred and twenty members. Who did the preaching? Fishermen. Think of it! A church of one hundred and twenty members has almost as many accessions as one of our leading denominations had last year with ten thousand churches working a whole year. Why? The apostles worked upon this faith: "It is not by might nor by power, but by my spirit, saith the Lord."

My method is and always will be to obtain immediate decision and open confession of Christ. I preach Christ. That is the sum and substance of my message. That cannot change. He alone can save. I hold fellowship with all who believe in Christ and follow Him as Lord and Master. My particular church is the Presbyterian and I was ordained as a Presbyterian minister. We Presbyterians know what we believe and why.

I believe in the absolute Deity of Jesus, His virgin birth, His atoning death, His resurrection from the dead, His future coming in glory, and the hopeless, helpless state of men aside from the redeeming work of Christ. We must never compromise with those who have apostatized from the truth if we are to be worthy sons and daughters of worthy ancestors who sealed their faith with their blood.

It seems incredible that we are living in a time when the Gospel is in the discard. The increasing spirit of liberalism and lackadaisical apathy on the part of the church and the increasing solidarity of the forces of evil lead me to the conclusion that America must turn to God to avoid a revolution. As former President Wilson said, "We must turn to God to avoid a world-wide revolution." The zero hour has arrived; for years they have been dynamiting the church in preparation for this modernistic war tank. I call the church back to the Bible. One reason why sin triumphs is because it is treated as though it were a cream puff instead of a rattlesnake.

The churches show the lowest type of spirituality they have shown in one hundred and twenty years. The churches are empty and the preachers are preaching to wood and varnish. The rationalistic semi-infidel preachers are one of the country's greatest curses.

The trouble with this country is her materialism. America has not and never will grow so rich and powerful but that she should fall on her knees and thank God for her material blessings. The church is losing ground. Where is there any living testimony of the power of Jesus to save that is being preached?

Our churches are as empty as last year's birds' nests. Religion has been reduced to an ethical code. An unfaithful church will always make an infidel world. We must make the church a magnet to draw the people. People do not go to church because it is their duty. The vast majority who go to church go because they want to go.

One reason why many do not believe in religion or go to church is because we are such caricatures of Christianity. The church was not manmade, but was organized by Jesus Christ for the purpose of carrying on Christian work. It reduces jails and penitentiaries and aids the police force, and in a thousand ways serves the state and nation.

The time has come when we preachers must be something more than walking theological mummies swathed in papyrus, oozing Greek diphthongs and seven terminologies of Latin and Greek extraction which can be intellectually digested only by those wearing alphabetical tails and appendages to their names. We must shell the woods for God.

This old God-hating, Christ-hating, whisky-soaked, Sabbath-breaking, blaspheming, adulterous, grafting, thieving, pleasure-loving, racketeering, socialistic, modernistic world is going to hell so fast she is breaking the speed limit. Come out with the church lifeboat: multitudes are drowning, the sea is covered with wrecks.

It is said, and my observation backs it up, that 10 per cent of the church membership cannot be found; 25 per cent seldom attend church; 50 per cent do not contribute to the work of the church; 75 per cent never attend prayer meeting, and 90 per cent do not have family prayer. The church is cursed with unbelief.

This world is horribly out of joint and must be brought under the omnipotent surgery of God. No glittering generalities, no rhetorical niceties. The message must ring out like a fire alarm. It must echo like a drumbeat before the battle. It must declare the whole counsel of God.

I am asked, "How long do you expect to preach?" I expect to preach as long as the blood pumps through my veins. I take the best of care of myself. I am careful of what I eat and how much. Half of what we eat is half more than we really need. Millions "eat their way into the grave." I am not much of a meat eater. I am not a vegetarian. I drink one or two quarts of milk a day and as much water.

I joined William Jennings Bryan's grape-juice brigade. I seldom eat before going to bed; but if I do, it is fruit or some of the many prepared foods. I am not a sound sleeper. I seldom go to bed before midnight.

It was said of Napoleon that he seldom slept more than four hours a night. For twenty-five years I was in Napoleon's class, but now I have learned to trust the Lord for rest and sleep. My faith has grown with my experience.

This is my debut as an author. I guess it will be my valedictory. I thank all my millions of friends who have aided and encouraged me in my struggles from the corn rows of Iowa.

To all who read these pages I urge with my closing words: Live the Christian life; men will admire you, women will respect you, little children will love you, and God will crown your life with success. And when the twilight of your life mingles with the purpling dawn of eternity, men will speak your name with honor and baptize your grave with tears when God attunes for you the evening chimes of life.

— The End —

Other Bur Oak Books of Interest

"All Will Yet Be Well"
The Diary of Sarah Gillespie
Huftalen, 1873–1952
By Suzanne L. Bunkers

The Folks
By Ruth Suckow

Letters of a German American Farmer
Jürnjakob Swehn Travels to America
By Johannes Gillhoff

My Vegetable Love
A Journal of a Growing Season
By Carl H. Klaus

Nothing to Do but Stay
My Pioneer Mother
By Carrie Young

Prairie Cooks
Glorified Rice, Three-Day Buns,
and Other Reminiscences
By Carrie Young with Felicia Young

Prairie Reunion
By Barbara J. Scot

A Ruth Suckow Omnibus
By Ruth Suckow

"A Secret to Be Burried"
The Diary and Life of Emily Hawley
Gillespie, 1858–1888
By Judy Nolte Lensink

Sarah's Seasons
An Amish Diary and Conversation
By Martha Moore Davis

Weathering Winter
A Gardener's Daybook
By Carl H. Klaus

The Wedding Dress
Stories from the Dakota Plains
By Carrie Young